Abraham
The Father of Us All

by Robert J. Koester

GWA
Books

ABRAHAM
THE FATHER OF US ALL
© 2026 Robert J. Koester
Cover Design: Pamela Clemons

Unless otherwise indicated, all Scripture quotations are from the Holy Bible, Evangelical Heritage Version ® (EHV ®) © 2017 Wartburg Project, Inc. All rights reserved. Used by permission. "EHV" and "Evangelical Heritage Version" are registered trademarks of Wartburg Project, Inc.

All rights reserved. No part of this book may be reproduced or transmitted in any form without the prior written permission of the publisher. Contact the publisher for permission to reprint or to use excerpts beyond fair use.

GWABooks.com
gwabooks@midco.net
3-26-3
ISBN: 978-1-7344319-9-5
Library of Congress Control Number: 2025923060

Table of Contents

Introduction v

Chapter 1   Genesis 11:27–12:9 1

   Abraham Travels From Ur to Canaan—11:27-32
   God Gives Abraham Far-reaching Promises—12:1-3
   Abraham Travels to Canaan—12:4-9

Chapter 2   Genesis 12:10–13:18................................... 25

   Abraham's Goes to Egypt—12:10-20
   Abraham and Lot Separate—13:1-17
   Abraham Builds Another Altar—13:18

Chapter 3   Genesis 14 49

   Abraham Rescues Lot—14:1-16
   Abraham Honors Melchizedek—14:17-24

Chapter 4   Genesis 15 65

   God Credits Righteousness to Abraham—15:1-7
   God Expands His Promise Regarding Canaan—15:8-21

Chapter 5   Genesis 16,17..83

   Ishmael Is Born—Chapter 16
   God Initiates Circumcision—Chapter 17

Chapter 6   Genesis 18 111

   God Renews His Promise to Abraham—18:1-15
   Abraham Prays for Lot—18:16-33

Chapter 7   Genesis 19 125

   God Answers Abraham's Prayer to Spare Lot—19:1-29
   It Is Dangerous to Live Close to Unbelief—19:30-38

Chapter 8   Genesis 20, 21 141

   Abraham Meets Abimelek, Part One—20:1-18
   God Fulfills His Promise: Isaac is born—21:1-21
   Abraham Meets Abimelek, Part Two—21:22-34

Chapter 9   Genesis 22:1-19 161

   God Tests Abraham—22:1-14
   God Renews His Promise to Abraham—22:15-19

Chapter 10   Genesis 23; 24; 25:1-8 193

   Abraham Prepares for Sarah's Future—Chapter 23
   Abraham Prepares for Isaac's Future—Chapter 24
   Abraham Prepares for His Own Future— 25:1-8

Summary 205

Scripture Index 215

References to Abraham in the New Testament 217

Introduction

Abraham is the father of the nation of Israel, whose story fills the pages of the Old Testament. But no other Old Testament figure has as prominent a place in the New Testament as Abraham. Abraham is the father of both the Jews and the Gentiles who share his faith in the Savior. Hence, the title of this book: "Abraham: The Father of Us All."

This book will look at the account of Abraham from four standpoints.

1. The account of Abraham is the account of God working to fulfill his promise of a Savior.

Scripture uses various words to describe God. Each chapter in this book will discuss one of those words. Those sections are titled "Keywords." We will not look at all the words Scripture uses to describe God. But the ones we have chosen correlate with the part of Abraham's life covered in that chapter. For example, Scripture's account of Abraham begins with God's name, the Lord. So it's natural that we focus on that word in chapter one.

2. In each chapter, we will cover a portion of the account of Abraham. Those sections are titled "The Life of Abraham."[1]

3. The New Testament refers to Abraham many times. We will look at all the places where it does that. In each chapter

---

[1] In Genesis 17, God changed Abraham's name. Up to that point, Moses calls him by his original name, Abram. After Genesis 17, Moses uses his new name, Abraham. In this book, we will always refer to him as Abraham.

of this book there are one or more sections titled "Abraham in the New Testament." There we will include all the New Testament references that correlate with the part of Abraham's life covered in that chapter. These references give us insights into Abraham's life, which the New Testament writers use to teach us about the Christian faith.

4. Abraham lived in a large household with many servants. They must have talked about what they saw going on around them. We will construct hypothetical conversations that these people may have had. Some of the speakers are real people, some are fictional. They discuss what was really happenng in Abraham's life, but the discussions themselves are fictional.

Martin Luther was not against speculating about what likely went on in Abraham's tent community. In one place, he spoke about the fact that Abraham "dared to make so long a journey with such a great number of people and cattle." He added, "It is amazing that so few of them were too weak or impatient to make the trip, and became mad at Abraham for not remaining in Haran or for not taking them to a more convenient place." [2]

When you come to "The Conversation" sections, don't think that the conversations are actually found in Scripture. They are there to help you imagine what life in Abraham's household might have been like and to think about what Abraham and Sarah's many servants and acquaintances likely discussed. Some conversations address issues that interpreters speculate about in their commentaries, so by placing the thoughts into

---

[2] Martin Luther, *Saemmtliche Schriften*, Vol. 1, (St. Louis: Concordia, 1889), p. 776.

fictional conversations, it becomes easier to distinguish fact from speculation.

In general, we will use the Evangelical Heritage Version (EHV). This is the recent translation produced by members of the Wisconsin Evangelical Lutheran Synod. However, we will sometimes use other translations. When we use a translation other than the EHV, we will note that in the reference. Other translations used are the English Standard Version (ESV), the New International Version, 1984 edition (NIV84), and the New International Version, 2011 edition (NIV11).

May the Lord bless your study and meditation on Abraham, the "father of us all."

Robert Koester

Chapter 1
Genesis 11:27–12:9

Abraham Travels from Ur to Canaan—11:27-32
God Gives Abraham Far-reaching Promises—12:1-3
Abraham Travels to Canaan—12:4-9

Prayer: Dear heavenly Father, you have promised that your Spirit is at work as I read and meditate on your Word. Therefore, help me read your Word not only for information, but as a source of the Spirit's strength. Give me your Holy Spirit as I read about Abraham. Shape my faith and life so that I more and more reflect the hope you have given me in Christ. Amen.

Keyword: the "Lord" [3]

Lord is the second word in the story of Abraham: "The Lord had said to Abram, 'Leave your country, your people and your father's household and go to the land I will show you'" (Genesis 12:1 NIV84). So the account of Abraham begins not with Abraham, but with "the Lord."

You have likely noticed that in English translations, the word is written "lord," "Lord," and "Lord."

When lord begins with a small "l," it refers to an important person. For example, some of Abraham's neighbors called

---

[3] The Hebrew word is יהוה.

him "lord" because they recognized him as a great man. Joseph's brothers called Joseph "lord" because of his position as ruler in Egypt.

But when lord refers to God, it is written in one of two ways: "Lord" (with a capital "L" and the last three letters in lower case), or LORD (with a capital L and "ORD" written in small capital letters). This is because in the original Hebrew, one of two different words can be behind the English translation. When the word is spelled Lord (the last three letters in lowercase) the Hebrew word is *adonai,* namely a great being. When the word is spelled LORD (the last three letters in small capitals) the Hebrew word is *yahweh,* which is a special name by which God wanted to be known.

To reflect this difference, English translators spell the English word differently. When God is called *adonai* in Hebrew, translators write "Lord." When God is called *Yahweh* in Hebrew, they write "LORD." [4]

The practical application for Bible reading is this: When you see "lord," you are seeing *adonai,* the Hebrew word for an exalted person or our exalted God. When you see "LORD," you are seeing *yahweh,* God's special name.

To summarize:

"lord" or "Lord": an exalted person or our exalted God.

---

[4] The Jewish people were afraid of pronouncing יהוה wrongly, thinking that if they did, they would be sinning against the second commandment, which forbids taking God's name in vain. So when they saw the four letters יהוה, they said "adonai" (a-doe-NIE. The last two letters are pronounced as they are in "lie"). As noted, this is the more general Hebrew word for lord, a great person or a great being, namely, God. For this reason, the actual pronunciation of יהוה, God's special name, is debated. Most pronounce it "YA-way." (The first "a" is short.) Sometimes translators use "Jehovah.".

CHAPTER 1   Genesis 11:27–12:9

"LORD:" God's special name for himself.

What does God's special name, the LORD (*yahweh*), mean, and why is it so important? Also, why is it such a wonderful word with which to begin the account of Abraham? Two episodes in the life of Moses will help us understand the meaning of *Jahweh*.

Jacob, Abraham's grandson, took his family of about seventy people from Canaan into Egypt, where they grew into a large nation. This account is found at the end of Genesis. The next book, Exodus, picks up the account at the point where God was ready to take Abraham's descendants out of Egypt and give them possession of Canaan, as he had promised Abraham. This is when God began to be known as "the LORD."

1) The first event was when God appeared to Moses in the wilderness and told him to lead Israel out of Egypt. God referred to himself as "the LORD." This name would encourage Moses to assume his role in delivering Israel, and it would encourage Israel to follow him and boldly conquer the land of Canaan:

> Then God spoke to Moses, telling him, "I am the LORD. I appeared to Abraham, to Isaac, and to Jacob, as God Almighty, but by my name, the LORD, I was not known to them. I also established my covenant with them, to give them the land of Canaan, the land where they were residing as aliens. I certainly have heard the groaning of the Israelites, whom the Egyptians have enslaved, and *I have remembered my covenant.*
>
> "Therefore, tell the Israelites, 'I am the LORD. I will bring you out from under the forced labor of the Egyptians. I will deliver you from being their slaves. I will

3

redeem you with an outstretched arm and with great acts of judgment. I will take you as my own people, and I will be your God. You will know that I am the LORD your God, the one who brought you out from under the forced labor of the Egyptians. I will bring you to the land which I swore with uplifted hand to give to Abraham, to Isaac, and to Jacob. I will give it to you as a possession. I am the LORD.'" (Exodus 6:2-8)

The significant phrase in this section is "I have remembered my covenant." After Adam and Eve sinned, God made a covenant with them and all mankind. The covenant was actually a promise. He would send a person to destroy Satan and undo what Satan had done when he used Adam and Eve to introduce sin into the world. He reaffirmed this promise to Abraham and gave him a role in its fulfillment. And God would use others along the way until the promise was fulfilled.

That's what *yahweh* (the LORD) means: God is faithful. He never forgets his promises, and he will undoubtedly fulfill them. He may seem inactive at times, but that never means he has decided to change or halt his plan of salvation.

God told Moses: "I have remembered my covenant" (Exodus 6:5). In Scripture, when we are told that God *remembered* something, it does not mean that God had forgotten about someone or something he planned to do. Rather, it means that God was getting ready to act in a new and different way. A good example of this is Noah. For months, Noah and his family floated in the ark on the waters of the flood. But at one point we are told that God "remembered Noah and all the beasts and all the livestock that were with him in the ark. And God made a wind blow over the earth, and the waters subsided" (Genesis 8:1). God remembered Noah in the sense that he (God) had been engaged in his destructive work, but now he was going to make the water go down so Noah and his family could safely leave the ark.

We can paraphrase what God said to Moses like this: "Abraham knew me only as the Promise Maker, not the Promise Fulfiller. But now, Moses, I am going to show myself as the Promise Fulfiller. It's been a long time since I promised to give Abraham's descendants the land of Canaan. But the time of waiting is over, and I'm going into action. You, Moses, will lead my people into the land that I, *Jehovah*, promised to give them."[5]

The second event tells us more about the meaning of the LORD. Sometime after God led the Israelites out of Egypt, Moses wanted to understand God better. So he asked God to show him his "glory,"[6] that is, the qualities that made him what he is. God responded by giving him a definition of his name:

> The LORD passed by in front of him and proclaimed: "The LORD, the LORD, the compassionate and gracious God, slow to anger, and overflowing with mercy and truth, maintaining mercy for thousands, forgiving guilt and rebellion and sin. He will by no means clear the guilty. He calls their children and their children's children to account for the guilt of the fathers, even to the third and the fourth generation." (Exodus 34:6,7)

---

[5] In the account of Abraham, several people used the name LORD. So it was not unknown to Abraham and others in his day. Note Abraham (14:22); Sarah (16:2); Abraham's servant (24:12); Rebekah's father, Bethuel, and her brother Laban (24:50,51).
[6] This word is often associated with "the Lord." In Hebrew it is כָּבוֹד. It is pronounced ka-VOD. (The "a" is short and the "o" is long.)

The glory of the Lord is his great qualities described in this passage: The Lord is "compassionate and gracious." He is "slow to anger," and he never stops showing "mercy and truth." He freely pours out his "mercy." He forgives every kind of sin. He punishes those who reject him by continuing to sin and incurring guilt. He limits his punishment to those who continue to rebel against him, just like their fathers did. But he graciously cuts short that time of punishment.

Abraham's life was a special time when the Lord's faithfulness to his promise of a Savior moved ahead quickly and decisively. Abraham laid the foundation for a new chapter in the Lord's plan to save the world and display his glory.

In New Testament times, God's name, the Lord, reminds us that he has faithfully fulfilled his promise of a Savior by sending his own Son to win forgiveness for all people, to forgive those who repent and believe, to build and protect his church, and to create a new heaven and earth where his people will live with him forever.

The Life of Abraham

Abraham Travels from Ur to Canaan—11:27-32

Abraham's father was named Terah. Terah and his family lived in the Chaldean city of Ur, in the modern-day country of Iraq. There are various opinions about the exact location of Ur, but many place it next to the Euphrates River, about 150 miles northwest of the present shoreline of the Persian Gulf.

Genesis mentions the following members of Terah's family: his son Abraham, Abraham's wife Sarah (whom we are told was barren and had no child), and Terah's grandson Lot, whose father Haran (another of Terah's sons) had already died in Ur. Terah took his family out of Ur and began a trip that took him around the top of the Fertile Crescent.[7]

We're told that Terah intended to go all the way to Canaan (Genesis 11:32). He traveled through Mesopotamia,[8] and continued west through the Fertile Crescent and into modern Syria. But he stopped about 400 miles north of Canaan and settled in a place called Haran.

In the New Testament, the deacon Stephen gave us more details. In his sermon to the Jewish leaders, he reminded them of how their nation began:

> Gentlemen, brothers and fathers, listen! The God of glory appeared to our father Abraham when he was in Mesopotamia, before he lived in Haran. God said to him, "Leave your land and your relatives and come to the land that I will show you." Then he left the land of the Chaldeans and settled in Haran. After his father died, God had him move from there to this land where you are now living. (Acts 7:2-4)

If we combine Stephen's and Moses' accounts, we learn that God appeared to Abraham himself in Ur and told him to go where he would lead him. Therefore, the impetus for the journey was not Terah's desire to move from Ur, but rather God's command to Abraham. We assume that Abraham told his father what God had said to him, and Terah then led his

---

[7] The Fertile Crescent is a large crescent-shaped piece of land starting at the Persian Gulf, arching north, then west into Syria and then south into the lands bordering the east shore of the Mediterranean Sea, including Canaan. People used this route for travel. Although traveling through the Fertile Crescent was longer, it was much easier than traversing the Arabian Desert, which lies in the center of the crescent.

[8] Mesopotamia means "the land between the rivers." It's a large section of land lying between the Tigris and Euphrates rivers. It stretches northwest from the Persian Gulf to modern-day Syria.

family out of Ur as God directed. For some reason, the group stopped short of Canaan and settled in Haran. Later, after his father died in Haran, God appeared to Abraham again and instructed him to complete the journey to Canaan.

Two facts come out in these verses that help us understand Abraham's life.

First, we are told that Sarah was barren and had not yet had a child. As we will see, God promised Abraham a son. But because Sarah was barren, it was humanly impossible for that to happen. For many years, God's promise of a child was their only source of hope. When God finally fulfilled his promise, it was clear to Abraham and Sarah that their son's birth was a miracle and that God alone was responsible for him.

Second, we are told that God had the family stop in Haran, where they lived until Terah died. By creating a place where most of Terah's family would remain and become its own community, God did two things.

He kept the main body of Terah's family relatively close to Abraham and provided Abraham and his son Isaac with a place to get wives for their sons. Both Abraham and Isaac were adamant that their sons not take wives from the idol-worshipping Canaanites living around them, and both sons found their wives from Abraham's relatives in Haran. See the account of Isaac's wife, Rebekah, in Genesis 24, and the account of Jacob's wives, Leah and Rachel, in Genesis 27:46 and Genesis 29:1-30.

The second thing he did by removing Abraham from Haran was to separate Abraham from the idol worship practiced by most people in the ancient world. This was not always the kind of idol worship practiced in large temples, before imposing statues, and directed by a corps of priests. It was often the worship of little images made from carved wood or stone, which families would set up and worship in their homes. These images might have represented the gods worshipped in the large, central temples.

Years later, some in Terah's family were still worshipping such images. We hear that Jacob's wife Rachel sinned in this regard (Genesis 31:34,35 and Genesis 35:2-4). If God had let Abraham's whole family continue into Canaan, these gods would have gone with them. But by keeping the main family in Haran and then commanding Abraham to leave there and continue to Canaan, God separated Abraham's family from his relatives' idol worship.

Yet Abraham's relatives in Haran knew the true God. Some, like Jacob's wife Rachel, still worshipped these images. But in the case of others, like Isaac's wife Rebekah and Jacob's wife Leah, we don't hear anything that implies they worshipped anyone except the true God.

Idolatry was no small matter, and this sin keeps coming up in Israel's history. Joshua, who many years later succeeded Moses as leader of the Israelites, spoke out about this horrible practice. He reminded them of what God had graciously done for Abraham:

> This is what the LORD, the God of Israel, has said: "From ancient times your ancestors, including Terah, who was the father of Abraham and the father of Nahor, lived beyond the Euphrates River, *and they served other gods*. But I took your father Abraham from across the River, and I caused him to walk through the whole land of Canaan. I multiplied his seed, and I gave Isaac to him." (Joshua 24:2,3)

But he seems to have despaired of the Israelites ever overcoming the practice. At the end of his final speech to them, Joshua commanded, "Now, therefore, fear the LORD and serve him wholeheartedly and faithfully. *Remove the gods that your fathers served in the region across the River and in Egypt, and serve the* LORD" (Joshua 24:14). Only if Joshua's generation worshipped the Lord as Abraham had would things go well for them. Only then could they play their role in God's fulfilling his promises to Abraham.

Was Abraham himself an idol worshipper before he left Ur? It is hard to say. Joshua refers to the "ancestors" of the Israelites. He says that "they" served other gods and names Terah. Yet he doesn't specifically say that Abraham or Nahor also practiced idol worship. [9] Since Joshua does not specifically implicate Abraham in idol worship, we might conclude that even in Ur, Abraham served the true God alone, and that when God removed him from Ur and then from Haran, God was removing him and his servants from his family's bad influence. I prefer that conclusion.

In one place, Isaiah encouraged the Israelites. He said that God would do for them what God had done for Abraham:

> Therefore this is what the LORD, *who redeemed Abraham*, says about the house of Jacob: Jacob will not be ashamed anymore. His face will not grow pale. But when his children see what I do among them, they will honor my name. They will honor the Holy One

---

[9] The situation is complicated by the fact that some people worshipped the true God *and* idols at the same time. For example, we know that Abraham's relative Laban and Laban's daughter Rachel worshipped idols (Genesis 31:25ff.). But Laban and his father, Bethuel, also worshipped the Lord (Genesis 24:50,51). If that was the case with Abraham, by separating him from Ur, God was leading him to worship him alone.

of Jacob. They will stand in awe of the God of Israel. (Isaiah 29:22-23)

Regardless of whether we think that Abraham worshipped idols, one thing is clear. God graciously separated Abraham from the idol worship his family practiced in Ur and in Haran. He called Abraham to himself (he "redeemed Abraham"), and he gave him a crucial role in his plan of salvation.

Terah died in Haran at 205 years old. After Terah died, the LORD appeared to Abraham again and said, "Get out of your country and away from your relatives and from your father's house and go to the land that I will show you" (Genesis 12:1). [10] Note the strong words the EHV uses there. Abraham was not just to leave Haran. He was to get out, get away, go to another place. This command might seem harsh until we reflect on the family's idol worship. God did not want idolatry to influence Abraham's family or servants in the days ahead.

God Gives Abraham Far-reaching Promises—12:1-3

Three things happen in these verses. First, God commanded Abraham to leave Haran. Second, God gave Abraham promises. And third, Abraham obeyed God and left Haran.

When reading this account, we sometimes focus on God's command and then immediately note Abraham's obedience—as if the main lesson in this account is that we should obey God like Abraham did. To be sure, that is an important lesson. But the main lesson revolves around the great

---

[10] The ESV translation reads, "Go from your country and your kindred and your father's house to the land that I will show you." This is accurate, but it lacks the force of the EHV translation.

promises God gave to Abraham. God's promises overcame the puzzling questions and hesitancy that were likely troubling Abraham after God told him to leave Haran. With these promises, Abraham could calm his fears, obey the Lord, and immediately leave Haran.

The same is true for us. God's promises, and not just his commands, pave the way for our obedience. Sometimes Christians get too preoccupied with God's commands—so preoccupied that we don't spend enough time with God's promises. But God's promises are the most important element in our obedience to him. When we remember all the blessings God has given us in Christ, we are prepared to obey God in everything.

Most people who move to a new place know where they are going and have a rough idea of what it will be like when they get there. Abraham didn't have that luxury. God simply told him to start a journey and follow his lead. But after God gave the command, he gave Abraham promises. With those promises in hand, Abraham could obey God's command, which he did.

Here are the promises God gave to Abraham:

I will make you a great nation.

>This promise gave Abraham all the hope and confidence he needed. God would put a wall around him and keep him from harm. He would not fall prey to marauding bandits or foreign kings.

I will bless you and make your name great.

>Abraham could expect his family to grow in numbers, and God would make him well-known to those around him. The miracles God later performed for Abraham's

descendants would also make their name great throughout the world.

You will be a blessing.

Not only would God bless Abraham, but he would also make Abraham a blessing to others. Abraham and Sarah might have wondered how God would fulfill this promise. Would others be blessed by watching Abraham become wealthier, wiser, and more powerful? Not likely. There must be something special about Abraham himself that would change their own lives for the better.

I will bless those who bless you, and I will curse anyone who dishonors you.

Abraham could leave Haran confident that his future would be safe. God would defend him in two ways. Everyone who blessed Abraham would be blessed by God in return. This would encourage people to be good to Abraham. And everyone who dishonored Abraham would incur God's anger. This would keep people from harming him.

We hear about this promise reflected in 1 Chronicles 16:20-22:

> They were wandering from nation to nation
> and from one kingdom to another people.
> Yet he did not permit anyone to oppress them.
> He rebuked kings on their account:
> "You must not touch my anointed ones.
> Against my prophets you must do no harm."

All of the families of the earth will be blessed in you.

This final blessing repeats the promise that Abraham would be a blessing to others, not just to the people living around him, but to everyone in the world. What is more, they would be blessed "in" Abraham. Something about Abraham himself—something that God would give him or make him become—would provide this worldwide blessing.

How all these promises would be fulfilled was likely a mystery to Abraham and Sarah. But as we will see, Abraham and Sarah had a clear understanding of God's promise of a Savior. All the promises of Genesis 12:2,3 can be interpreted in the light of that one, great promise.

Abraham Travels to Canaan—12:4-9

Abraham was already seventy-five years old when he left Haran. He took with him his wife Sarah, his nephew Lot, his servants, and his possessions. The trip from Haran to the border of Canaan was about 400 miles, not a quick trip for an older couple and their possessions.

Abraham's group was large. We hear that he had 318 servants trained for battle, who had been born in his household (Genesis 14:14). Since that event took place within the first 15 years of Abraham's life in Canaan (see Genesis 16:16), these 318 people would have already been growing up in the homes of Abraham's servants when he left Haran.

This helps us envision Abraham's entourage. We shouldn't picture Abraham, Sarah, and Lot, followed by a few servants, sheep, and goats. Rather, we should envision a large group of people, stretching out over a long distance, with a camp the size of a small town.

Abraham traveled south into Canaan. This was not an open, unoccupied place. Moses wrote, "The Canaanites were in the land at that time," a powerful people, most of whom worshipped idols (Genesis 12:6). Years later, when God told Abraham's descendants to take possession of Canaan, most of them were deathly afraid of the Canaanites and refused to trust in God's power to conquer them. They said to their leader, Moses,

> The people who live in the land are strong, and the cities are fortified and very large. We also saw the descendants of Anak there. The Amalekites are living in the land of the Negev. The Hittites, the Jebusites, and the Amorites are living in the hill country. The Canaanites are living by the sea and along the Jordan. . . . We are not able to go up against the people, because they are stronger than we are." (Numbers 13:28-31)

The Canaanites might not have been as powerful in Abraham's day as they were in Moses' day, but they were not to be taken lightly. As Abraham traveled south, he must have seen powerful cities and the people of the land looking at him with suspicion, wondering what these newcomers were up to. But this was where the Lord appeared to Abraham and said, "I will give this land to your descendants" (Genesis 12:7). So what did Abraham do? He didn't react like the Israelites mentioned above. He "built an altar to the Lord and proclaimed the name of the Lord" (Genesis 12:7). Right there, out in the open, for all to see.

There must have been more people at Abraham's altars than just Abraham, Sarah, Lot, and a few others. Based on the number of servants born in his household, the group might have numbered a thousand or more. When Abraham worshipped the Lord, he likely talked about God's promise of a Savior and the related promises God had made to him. Among his servants were many who shared their master's faith and way of life, even servants he had acquired from the nations around him. This assumption is based on what happened later when God instituted the covenant of circumcision (Genesis 17:9,10). At that time God commanded Abraham to circumcise his entire household: "Every boy among you who is eight days old shall be circumcised, every male throughout your generations, whether he is born in your house or purchased with money from any foreigner who is not descended from you" (Genesis 17:12). It is unlikely that God would have made this command if Abraham's household had remained ignorant of God's promises to Abraham and did not share his faith, of which circumcision was a sign. They must have been gathering around Abraham's altars for some time and listening as he described the true God.

We are told that Abraham "proclaimed [or called on] the name of the Lord" (Genesis 12:8). What truths about God did he speak of? Was it that God existed and was much more powerful than any of the world's gods? Was it a general confidence that God is love? Was it the conviction that if they served God, then God would bless them?

From everything we learn about Abraham, his faith went far beyond general truths. It was specific. He believed in a Savior from sin. Almost immediately after Adam and Eve sinned, God said to Satan, "I will put hostility between you and the woman, and between your seed and her seed. He will crush your head, and you will crush his heel" (Genesis 3:15). The woman's seed would erase the guilt of sin and take down the barrier between God and human beings. This promise was at the center of the faith of all Old Testament believers, just as it is for us.

We can reinforce this truth by looking at some other Old Testament figures.

Faith in God's promise spelled the difference between righteous Abel and wicked Cain. The writer of Hebrews says, "By faith Abel offered a better sacrifice to God than Cain did. By faith he was commended in Scripture as righteous; God testified favorably about his gifts. And by faith he still speaks, even though he is dead" (Hebrews 11:4). If Abel continues to speak on behalf of New Testament believers, then his faith must have been the same as ours.

One of the pre-flood patriarchs, Enoch, shared Abraham's faith:

> By faith Enoch was taken up, so that he would not experience death, and he was not found because God took him away. In fact, before he was taken away, he was commended in Scripture as one who "pleased God." And without faith it is impossible to please God. Indeed, it is necessary for the one who approaches God to believe that he exists and that he rewards those who seek him. (Hebrews 11:5,6)

Enoch believed in the true God and sought his blessings. The writer of Hebrews uses Enoch's example to encourage us in the New Testament. This shows that his faith was the same as ours, even though we know much more about the Savior's life.

Faith spelled the difference between righteous Noah and the people of the world, whose wickedness was great. The writer of Hebrews says, "By faith Noah, when he was warned about things that had not been seen before, built an ark, in reverent fear, in order to save his family. By it he condemned the world and became an heir of the righteousness that is by faith" (Hebrews 11:7).

Noah believed that God would judge the world, just as we do. He built an ark and trusted that God would save him, just as we trust that God will save us on the last day. Through faith in God's Word, he was considered righteous by God, just as we are.

The point is this: The New Testament writers would not have used the faith of Old Testament believers if their faith was different from ours—if it was not centered on God's promise of a Savior, as ours is. They understood such things as right and wrong, judgment and salvation, and knew that their sacrifices were not just gifts to God but offered in view of the promised Savior's own sacrifice.

Understanding this about Abraham helps us identify with him and learn from him. It also helps us understand why Abraham is such an important figure in the New Testament and why Jesus and its writers so often use him to teach us.

Getting back to Abraham's worship services. When we envision those worship services, we should see not only the large group of people gathered around Abraham's altars. We should also listen to him speaking about his faith in the Savior and defining his service to God in that context.

When he built his first altar, God had just told him something he had wondered about for a long time, namely, where God was leading him. After praising God for his promises and offering him sacrifices, Abraham might have explained what God just revealed to him: "God had told me—and you too—to follow his lead. But he did not tell me where he was leading us. Now he has revealed that to us. It is to this place, to this beautiful country of Canaan." Abraham would have spoken about God's promises to help and protect him. He would have asked for God's continued protection—not just for his own sake but also for the sake of his household. And he would have also asked God to protect him for the sake of all mankind, who would be blessed through the Savior who would come from him.

Abraham continued to travel south, pitching his tent between two Canaanite cities, Bethel and Ai. Again, we hear that "he built an altar to the LORD and proclaimed [or called on] the name of the LORD" (Genesis 12:8).

Abraham in the New Testament

John 8:56-58

> [56] Your father Abraham was glad that he would see my day. He saw it and rejoiced." [57] The Jews replied, "You aren't even fifty years old, and you have seen Abraham?" [58] Jesus said to them, "Amen, Amen, I tell you: Before Abraham was born, I am."

Jesus rebuked the religious leaders of his day for rejecting him and claiming that they were children of Abraham. Jesus said that if the Jews really were children of Abraham, they would have treasured him, the promised Savior Jesus, just like Abraham did. Abraham's faith was not a general faith in God. It was faith in the coming Savior, in Jesus himself. What's more, Jesus would know this better than anyone. He existed when Abraham lived, and long before that!

Acts 3:24-26

> [24] "All the prophets from Samuel on, as many as have spoken, have talked about these days. [25] You are the

sons of the prophets and of the covenant that God made with our fathers when he said to Abraham: 'In your seed all the families of the earth will be blessed.' ²⁶ "God raised up his Servant and sent him to you first, to bless you by turning every one of you away from your wicked ways."

The Jewish people were the primary recipients of the promises God made with Abraham. They were the first ones to whom Jesus and the apostles spoke the message of repentance and faith.

Abraham was also a blessing to all the people in the world. This was already true in Abraham's day, when many non-Israelites came to faith. It was especially true in the New Testament when God sent missionaries to the Gentiles (the non-Jews).

Hebrews 11:8

⁸ By faith Abraham obeyed when he was called to go to a place that he was going to receive as an inheritance, and he left without knowing where he was going.

Abraham left Haran "by faith." His act was not merely obedience to a command. It was primarily an act of faith, based on God's promises.

What we learn about Abraham from the New Testament: Abraham's faith was in the promised Savior, and he rejoiced when he thought about his birth. Although some of God's promises to Abraham (like the physical land of Canaan) applied only to Abraham's descendants, God had promised that through Abraham all nations would be blessed.

CHAPTER 1   Genesis 11:27–12:9

The Conversation

We're assuming that Abraham's servants talked about what they heard at Abraham's altar. This conversation is between four of Abraham's servants. Both the people and the conversation are fictional.

The characters:

Caleb: A servant of Abraham and a mature believer in the true God.

Chloe: Caleb's wife, also a mature believer in the true God.

Abihu: A man who is somewhat skeptical about Abraham's faith.

Anna: Abihu's wife, who shares Abihu's thoughts.

> *Caleb:* That cleared up a lot for me.
>
> *Chloe:* Now I know what Abraham has been doing these past months—and where he's been leading us.
>
> *Caleb:* He's been following God's lead. God didn't tell him where he was to go. But now Abraham knows. This will be his land.
>
> *Abihu:* I still don't see the fairness in this. There we were, living in nice brick homes—maybe not the best, but better than these tents. We got up each day, did our jobs, and went home. We could put our kids to bed and not have them complain about sleeping on the ground.
>
> *Anna:* And believe me, all they do is complain. "What's going to happen tomorrow?" "Do we have to get up early again?" "I hate packing everything up."

Abihu: And the walking. All the walking! Have you ever tried to get your kids to walk a mile? Now it's all day.

Caleb: We've had our problems, too.

Anna interrupts: And we don't even know where we're going. We pass a Canaanite town, and they look at us like a bunch of outsiders, intruding on their property! Why are we here, they wonder. Maybe we're scouting the place for a raiding party coming behind us.

Chloe: Anna, like Caleb said, we've had our problems too. And yes, the look on the faces of those Canaanite farmers scares me too. I don't blame them. They have no idea what we're doing here. We *are* outsiders!

But now it makes sense. Abraham himself didn't know where he was going either. God had withheld that from him—until now.

Caleb: When he built that altar and asked us to join him, we started to realize the difficulties he and Sarah were facing. "Go to a land that I will show you," said God. "You will feel vulnerable to attack. You may not know the safest route to take. But I will be with you. I will show you the way."

Chloe: And the promises God gave him! They're almost unbelievable. Incomprehensible blessings. Absolute protection against his enemies.

Caleb: And the promise that God will bless those who bless Abraham. That sounds good. I'll serve Abraham the best I can. Maybe the Lord will bless me, too.

Abihu: What was that he said—that all nations would be blessed through him? Sounds a little pompous to me. How do we know that Abraham's God is really as powerful as Abraham thinks? We took some household gods along with us. We pray to them every night. What about them? Should we just throw them out?

Caleb: Yes, that would be a good start.

Closing

First Chronicles 16:8-36 is a psalm written by David. In this psalm, David praised God for giving Abraham the land of Canaan and for protecting him during the years he lived there as a foreigner.

1 Chronicles 16:18-28

> To you [Abraham] I will give the land of Canaan,
>   as your portion for an inheritance."
> When you were few in number,
>   of little account,
>   and sojourners in it,
> wandering from nation to nation,
>   from one kingdom to another people,
> he allowed no one to oppress them;
>   he rebuked kings on their account,
> saying, "Touch not my anointed ones,
>   do my prophets no harm!"
> Sing to the Lord, all the earth!
> Tell of his salvation from day to day.
> Declare his glory among the nations,
>   his marvelous works among all the peoples!
> For great is the Lord, and greatly to be praised,
>   and he is to be feared above all gods.
> For all the gods of the peoples are worthless idols,
>   but the Lord made the heavens.
> Splendor and majesty are before him;
>   strength and joy are in his place.

ABRAHAM

Ascribe to the LORD, O families of the peoples,
ascribe to the LORD glory and strength!

Chapter 2
Genesis 12:10–13:18

Abraham Goes to Egypt—12:10-20
Abraham and Lot Separate—13:1-17
Abraham Builds Another Altar—13:18

Prayer: Dear heavenly Father, we come before you with joy in our hearts because you have included us among the descendants of Abraham. Help us view our time on earth and our possessions like Abraham viewed his. Give us confidence to know that since you are King over all things, you will supply everything we need to do your work. Amen.

Keyword: "Righteousness" [11]
Part One: God's Righteousness

In the last chapter, we looked at the word "Lord." In this chapter, we will look at the word "righteousness." Righteousness is one of the Lord's chief characteristics.

In this book, we are going to look at the word righteousness four times. Although the word itself occurs only twice in the

---

[11] The Hebrew word for righteousness is צְדָקָה. It is pronounced tsu-da-KAH. All the vowels are short.

account of Abraham, the idea of righteousness occurs in two other contexts.

In this chapter, we will look at God's own righteousness. In Genesis 14, we will see that Christ won the gift of righteousness for all people. In Genesis 15, we will see that God gives us the gift of Christ's righteousness through faith. Later, in Genesis 22, we will focus on Abraham's own deeds of righteousness—things he did because he trusted God and wanted to obey him. There, we'll also think about our own lives of righteousness.

Righteousness contains the word "right." God is righteous because he always does the right thing. He has expressed his will in the Ten Commandments, and he always follows his own will when he guides and shapes what happens among the nations of the world and in the lives of people.

In Scripture, however, God's righteousness is often used in a special way. It still refers to the fact that God is right in everything he does in regard to his promise of a Savior. It is about keeping his promise of a Savior on track. It is about calling people to faith, keeping them in the faith, and successfully bringing them to Heaven.

The following passages talk about the righteousness of God in this special sense. As you read them, note the words describing God that surround the word righteousness. They help us get a fuller and more wonderful understanding of what it means that God is righteous.

Isaiah 42:6-8

Here God is appointing the Savior to carry out his will to save all people:

> I am the Lord.

I have called you in *righteousness*.
I will hold on to your hand,
and I will guard you.
I will appoint you to be a covenant for the people,
to be a light for the nations,
to open the eyes of the blind,
to bring the prisoners out from the dungeon,
and to bring those who sit in darkness out of prison.
I am the Lord; that is my name.
I will not give my glory to another,
nor my praise to idols.

Here is August Pieper's explanation of the righteousness of God in the above passage:

> Righteousness is the source from which the acts of the Lord flow concerning the Servant—taking Him by the hand, watching over Him, making Him to be a covenant for the people, and the Light of the gentiles. Thus righteousness can be nothing other than the Lord's will to save, His zeal for the salvation of Israel. . . . It is difficult, perhaps impossible, to express with one English word all that righteousness conveys, for while the word here and elsewhere denoted especially the Lord's purpose to save, it also includes the objective salvation itself together with its preparation and ultimate goal.[12]

The Savior proclaimed God's righteousness:

Psalm 40:9,10

I proclaim *righteousness* in the great assembly;
I do not seal my lips,
as you know, O Lord.
I do not hide your *righteousness* in my heart;
I speak of your *faithfulness* and *salvation*.

---

[12] From August Pieper, *Isaiah II*, (Milwaukee, Northwestern Publishing House, 1979) p. 185. The English word righteousness has been substituted for Pieper's use of the Hebrew.

I do not conceal your *love* and your *truth*
from the great assembly.

Here, the psalmist relates what Jesus said about the righteous acts God did for the people of his day. Note the words that surround the word righteousness: faithfulness, salvation, love, and truth.

In the following passages, a similar cluster of words surrounds God's righteousness :

Psalm 36:5-12

>   Lord, your *mercy* reaches to the heavens.
>   Your *faithfulness* to the skies.
>   Your *righteousness* is as high as the mountains of God.
>   Your *justice* is as deep as the ocean.
>   You *save* both man and animal, O Lord.
>   How precious is your *mercy*, O God!
>   So all people find refuge in *the shadow of your wings*.
>   They are satisfied by *the rich food* of your house.
>   You let them drink from your *river of delights*.
>   For with you is *the fountain of life*.
>   In *your light* we see light.
>   Stretch out your *mercy* over those who know you,
>   your *righteousness* to the upright in heart.
>   Do not let the foot of the proud trample me.
>   Do not let the hand of the wicked drive me away.
>   *There the evildoers have fallen.*
>   They have been thrown down.
>   They are not able to rise!

Abraham and Sarah likely wondered more than once about the mysteries in their lives: Why Canaan? Why Lot's problems? Why wait so long for a son? Why the difficulties they faced with the residents of the land? How could there still be some believers among the idol-worshipping Canaanite population? In future chapters, we'll come across the events that spurred these questions. But because of God's righteousness in fulfilling his promises, Abraham and Sarah could be sure that God was always doing the right thing at the right time.

The story of Abraham is the story of God's righteousness in action. God promised to make Abraham into a large nation. He set Abraham and his descendants apart from the rest of the nations and gave them the land that would someday be the birthplace of the Savior. In righteousness he faithfully blessed and protected Abraham and his family until the Savior was born.

The Life of Abraham

Abraham Goes to Egypt—Genesis 12:10-20

From Bethel and Ai, where Abraham built his second altar, he traveled southward into the Negev. The Negev is the southern, more desertlike section of Canaan, which becomes more arid as one continues south. However, Abraham had to leave there because of a severe famine. He traveled south into Egypt, which usually had a supply of food. The Egyptians could irrigate their fields with the water of the Nile River that flowed through the land.

At that time in history, Egypt was a very powerful nation. When Abraham entered Egypt, he was afraid that if the Egyptians knew that Sarah was his wife, someone might kill him and take her. So Abraham told Sarah to say that she was his sister. He reasoned that if an Egyptian prince wanted Sarah, his life would be spared. And what's more, the Egyptians would treat him well.

The Pharaoh himself (the Egyptian name for the king of Egypt) took Sarah as his wife. And he gave Abraham many gifts for Sarah's sake.

We are not explicitly told that God kept Pharaoh from consummating the marriage. But everything points in that direction. In those days, powerful rulers had harems where their wives and concubines lived for a period of time before they were brought to the king. (An example of this custom is found in Esther 2:12,13, where Esther's time of preparation lasted a full year.) That's where Sarah was likely taken—to prepare her for Pharaoh's bed. However, as soon as Sarah entered Pharaoh's court, the Lord "inflicted serious diseases on Pharaoh and his household because of Abram's wife Sarai" (Genesis 12:17). These diseases likely brought Pharaoh's marriage plans to a halt.

Abraham's lie might have been more serious than he realized. At this time, Abraham did not seem to have known that the promised son had to come from Sarah. In chapter 15, when God renewed his promise of a son, he simply told Abraham that "a son coming from your own body will be your heir" (Genesis 15:4). Later, Sarah and Abraham tried to fulfill God's promise through a union between Abraham and Hagar, Sarah's maidservant. It is hard to imagine that Abraham and Sarah would have done that if they had known that Sarah would be the child's mother.

It wasn't until a year before the child was born that God made it clear that he would come from Sarah. At that time he said, "As for Sarai your wife, you are no longer to call her Sarai; her name will be Sarah. I will bless her and will surely give you a son by her. I will bless her so that she will be the mother of nations; kings of peoples will come from her" (Genesis 17:15,16). Even when he heard that, Abraham objected. He said to God, "If only Ishmael [his son by Hagar] might live under your blessing!" (Genesis 17:18). God had to repeat what he just said about Sarah, "Yes, but your wife Sarah will bear you a son, and you will call him Isaac. I will establish my covenant with him as an everlasting covenant for his descendants after him" (Genesis 17:19).

A far as Moses tells us, when Abraham was in Egypt, he likely didn't realize that Sarah would, in fact, be the mother of the promised son. Therefore, his action was putting God's promise in danger. If Pharaoh had consummated the marriage, Sarah's relationship to Abraham would have been thrown into turmoil. Even if Sarah had remained barren and not had a child by Pharaoh, Pharaoh might not have given Sarah back to Abraham. And he might have punished Abraham in some way for lying to him. If Abraham had been killed or permanently separated from Sarah, humanly speaking, the fulfillment of God's promise would have been in jeopardy.

There were other consequences of Abraham's lie. Abraham became more of a hypocrite day by day as he thanked Pharaoh for the flocks, herds, and servants Pharaoh was giving him as his new brother-in-law. To protect Abraham and Sarah and keep his promise of a Savior on track, God afflicted Pharaoh and his household with terrible pain, which they would not have had to suffer if Abraham had not lied about Sarah.

What is more, Abraham had completely misjudged Pharaoh. Pharaoh would never have taken Sarah had he known that she was Abraham's wife. What Abraham did was unfair.

Somehow—we are not told how—Pharaoh came to realize that the diseases his household was suffering were miraculous, and that Abraham's God had sent them because Pharaoh had taken a married woman into his home.

None of this reflected well on Abraham or the Lord. Pharaoh immediately rebuked Abraham for lying to him and ejected him, along with Sarah, Lot, and his servants, from Egypt. Yet even though Abraham was at fault, God rebuked Pharaoh and protected Abraham in line with the promises he had made to him.

Abraham, Sarah, Lot, and their servants left Egypt and went back to Canaan. They traveled through the Negev, the dry southern region of Canaan. Later, Abraham would settle in the Negev and make his home there (Genesis 20:1).

Abraham returned to the place where he had built his second altar, between Bethel and Ai, and called on the name of the Lord. He likely thanked God for the promises God made when he told Abraham to leave Haran. But now he had more to be thankful for. In Egypt, Abraham had experienced God's protecting hand in a very striking way. Abraham had potentially derailed God's promise. He saw God's great power and could thank God for keeping the promise on track.

Also, he might have publicly confessed his sin, both for his own sake and for the sake of his servants, to help them better understand sin and God's forgiveness.

The Conversation

One night on their way home, Caleb, Chloe, and a new character, Merit, talked about what they had just experienced in Egypt. What Caleb says is a sample of how Martin Luther interpreted Abraham's lie about Sarah. Interpreters sometimes say that in lying, Abraham was sinning, and there is no other way to evaluate his actions. But Luther did the opposite. Namely, he tried to put what Abraham did in the best possible light. Luther, however, does this almost to a fault, and many disagree with him.

In this conversation, Caleb will interpret Abraham's lie about Sarah as Martin Luther did. [13] As you listen to this conversation, think about how you yourself would interpret what Abraham did. As you do this, keep in mind that Scripture itself always describes Abraham as a man of faith and is never critical of what he does.

The characters:

Caleb: A servant of Abraham and a mature believer in the true God.

Chloe: Caleb's wife, also a mature believer in the true God.

Merit: One of the servants Pharaoh gave to Abraham.

> *Chloe:* Our life was going so well in Egypt. It was permanent and peaceful. But it was all a lie. Why did Abraham do it? He has God's promise to protect him. Sarah was his wife! Not his sister. I don't understand.

---

[13] Martin Luther, *Luther's Works*, Vol. 2, (St. Louis, Concordia Publishing House, 1960), pp. 287-323.

Caleb: Not so fast, Chloe. It is easy to get down on Abraham. But how harsh should we be toward our master Abraham? True, he lied about Sarah, and he made Sarah lie about herself. But think of the pressure he was under. He couldn't go back to Haran, much less to Ur. He needed food. His only option was to stay in Egypt.

Chloe: No one faults Abraham for that.

Caleb: But consider what was at stake: It is said that rulers in Egypt will kill a man to get his wife. Abraham knew that God's promise of a son required that he, Abraham, stay alive. If he had knowingly put himself in danger, he would have been testing God: "Let's see if you will keep me alive." I agree that he lied, but it was a legitimate lie because he told it to protect God's promise that he would be a blessing to the whole world. After all, Abraham could have had a son by someone other than Sarah. Sarah knew her husband would pray for her, and she was confident that God would protect her too.

Chloe: But why didn't he just pray that God would protect him and the promise? Why did he push Sarah into harm's way?

Caleb: Chloe, I admit, you make a good point. Abraham's faith may have faltered a bit and he may have committed a sin of weakness. But Abraham was a man of great faith. I would rather focus on that. He was only trying to keep the promise safe. He did it all to the glory of God and for the good of the world.

Chloe: All I can say is this: If I were Sarah, I would have refused.

Caleb: Dear Chloe, it was to her credit that she didn't. She shared the faith of her husband and trusted that God would work things out according to his gracious will.

Merit, jumping into the conversation: OK. Stop there for a moment. Who says that Abraham might have been killed?

Caleb: It's been known to happen in Egypt and in other places.

Merit: But does that mean it always happens? And let me ask you this: Has this Pharaoh ever killed anyone to get a wife?

Chloe: And is it right to assume such things about people we don't even know?

Caleb: Yes, Chloe, we must make those assumptions. You can't always judge a person on the basis of what they've done in the past. My master understands the sinfulness of human nature, just like we all do. Even if Pharaoh never killed anyone for his wife, it didn't mean that he might not kill Abraham to get Sarah. Abraham was wise not to take the chance.

Merit: Look what came out of this. Pharaoh and my people were innocent, but God afflicted them on account of Sarah.

Caleb: The situation required it. True, Pharaoh was innocent, and what he did was lawful. But did he investigate the facts of the matter as carefully as he should have? He was, in fact, taking a married woman as his wife, and that was wrong. God had to afflict Pharaoh for Pharaoh's own good, to warn and teach him. And to Pharaoh's credit, he realized that God was trying to tell him something by these diseases. And he quickly figured out what that was.

Merit: So what are you saying? That this whole terrible event was for the good of my people?

Caleb: Think about it. Consider how it all turned out. At first, Pharaoh was angry. But if I know Abraham, he talked to Pharaoh about God's promises. He likely explained why he had lied about Sarah. Everyone knows that powerful people often act like tyrants. He may have urged Pharaoh to accept God's rebuke. I think Pharaoh came to faith. He realized that Abraham was a great man through whom God would bless the world. He came to fear God, and he humbled himself. He sent Abraham away because he was afraid that someone else in his kingdom might harm Abraham. Anyway, that is what I think happened.

Chloe: Caleb, I admit that we don't know everything Abraham was thinking—things that might shed a better light on Abraham's lie. I admit that everything turned out well—for Abraham, for Sarah, and for us too. But I'm not convinced that he's quite as innocent as you make him out to be.

Luther's interpretation is often dismissed. But the simple fact that God rebuked Pharaoh even though he was innocent, but did not rebuke Abraham even though he was guilty of lying, raises the question: Might there be some reason that justified Abraham for saying that Sarah was his sister?

Some tend to overemphasize the sins of God's people. Their discussion ends with the statement: Scripture is showing that the great men and women of old are sinful like the rest of us and need God's forgiveness like all believers do. This is true. But might there be more? Luther demonstrates a gracious spirit that always saw God's people in the best possible light. In doing that, he imitated Scripture. He focused on Abraham's concern for God's promises and claimed that Abraham lied to protect those promises rather than because he was afraid.

Luther probably went too far in that direction. But at the very least, he forces us to rethink the matter.

The Life of Abraham

Abraham and Lot Separate—Genesis 13:1-17

God promised to bless Abraham. And he promised to pass that blessing along: "I will bless those who bless you" (Genesis 12:3). That had come true for Lot.

But God's blessings led to conflict. As long as the two lived close together, there was not enough grazing land for their flocks and herds, and likely not enough water. So their herdsmen quarreled.

Conflicts are always sad. But they are inevitable, even in the lives of believers. For believers, the main question is always "How can I solve this conflict in a God-pleasing way?" That was Abraham's concern. But before we look at how Abraham did that, we should get to know Lot.

Abraham had many problems. We just saw an example, namely, Abraham's struggles in Egypt, where he had to live as a stranger among people he felt he could not trust.

But other problems arose within his family, and Lot caused some of the more serious ones. In brief, Abraham had to watch Lot make choices driven by worldly concerns and suffer for those choices.

Starting with this episode, Moses records other times when Lot's worldly choices brought danger and sadness into his life. These were dark times for Abraham, and they brought danger and sadness into his life as well. Once, he risked his own life for Lot. On another occasion, Abraham endured an intense spiritual struggle on Lot's account, wrestling with God in prayer to spare Lot's life.

Abraham loved Lot. Abraham acknowledged Lot as his brother (Genesis 13:9) in faith. And God also loved him. The apostle Peter spoke about God's love for Lot. In his second book, Peter wrote,

> If he rescued righteous Lot, greatly distressed by the sensual conduct of the wicked (for as that righteous man lived among them [the people of Sodom] day after day, he was tormenting his righteous soul over their lawless deeds that he saw and heard); then the Lord knows how to rescue the godly from trials, and to keep the unrighteous under punishment until the day of judgment. (2 Peter 2:7-9)

At first, we are tempted to think that Lot was an unbeliever. Indeed, Lot did things that might lead us to think that. But, as Peter says, Lot was righteous through faith, just as Abraham was righteous through faith. Peter says that God delivered him from the wickedness of Sodom and preserved him for Heaven.

We return to the quarrel between Lot's and Abraham's herdsmen. It was evident that they had to separate the flocks and herds. But Abraham did not want to quarrel. He knew that quarreling produces anger and bitterness, and he wanted none of that.

Moses notes that the land was filled with unbelievers: "The Canaanites and Perizzites were also living in the land at that time" (Genesis 13:7). It is never good when unbelievers see believers quarreling. In chapter 15, we will hear that God was still giving the residents of Canaan time to repent of their sins (Genesis 15:16) before he used the Israelites to destroy them. That goal would have been harmed if the Canaanites were forced to watch a fight between two servants of the true God, the God they should have been worshipping. Moreover, if the Canaanites saw a conflict within Abraham's own camp, they might have been emboldened to attack him.

Most importantly, Abraham wanted to base his life on God's promises. He could have pulled rank on Lot and demanded the best land for himself. But he didn't. He trusted God's promise that the entire land would eventually belong to him and his descendants. So he deferred to Lot and let him make the choice.

Lot let his greed guide him. He moved down to the fertile plain of the Jordan River Valley. It seems that for a time, he continued to live outside of Sodom in tents near his herdsmen. The next time we meet him, however, he is living inside the city of Sodom. We don't know why Lot moved there, but it may have been for the same worldly reason he chose to live near Sodom. There, he could better carry out his business of selling animals to the people of the city for food and clothing. But as we will see, it was a tragic move. The people of Sodom were "wicked and were sinning greatly against the Lord" (Genesis 13:13).

Immediately after Lot left for the rich plain around the Jordan River, God reaffirmed two of the promises he had made to Abraham. First, he promised to give Abraham and his descendants the entire land of Canaan. It's as if he were saying to Abraham, "You let Lot choose the best land for himself. You did that because you knew you would never lose what I promised to give you."

God told Abraham to look in every direction, even toward the east, where Lot was heading. That land would someday belong to him. God then told Abraham to travel through the land to see it firsthand. It would impress on Abraham what a tremendous promise God had made to him.

When we think about Abraham's trip through the land of Canaan, our thoughts are drawn to the future when some of his descendants made a similar trip. God had fulfilled his promise to Abraham: "I will make your offspring like the dust of the earth" (Genesis 12:16). When God was ready to give them the land of Canaan, their leader, Moses, told twelve of Israel's leaders to walk throughout the land and survey it. He urged them to have courage and trust God like Abraham had. He said to them,

> Go up this way through the Negev and go up into the hill country. See what the land is like. See if the people who live in the land are strong or weak. See if they are few or many. See if the land that they live in is good or bad. See what kind of cities they live in. See if the cities are camps or fortified places. See what the land is like. See if the land is fertile or poor. See if there are trees in the land or not. Be courageous and bring back some of the fruit of the land. (Numbers 13:17-20)

Sadly, most of the leaders did not have Abraham's confidence in God's promise. The scouts reported that powerful people lived there, and they expressed doubt that they could defeat them. But two of the scouts, Caleb and Joshua, reflected Abraham's certain hope: "We should go up now and take possession of it, because we can certainly conquer it!" (Numbers 13:30). Sadly, the people followed the advice of the doubters and refused to trust in the Lord. Abraham's descendants had to wait another 38 years for God to fulfill his promise to a new generation.

The Conversation

This conversation is between one of Abraham's servants and one of Lot's servants. They are on different sides of the dispute over the grazing land, but they remain friends and discuss what would soon happen. The characters and the conversation are hypothetical.

The characters:

Caleb: A mature believer in the true God and one of Abraham's servants.

Lamech: A mature believer in the true God and one of Lot's servants.

> *Caleb:* It's been a rough year for both Abraham and Lot, hasn't it, Lamech?
>
> *Lamech:* Indeed. But we've been part of the problem too, haven't we, Caleb?
>
> *Caleb* laughing: Actually, it's the Lord who's caused the problem. If he'd quit blessing our masters, things would be fine. But when the herds almost double each year, it's hard to keep them watered and fed.

Lamech: I don't know what Abraham and Lot can do except go their own ways and find the pasture we both need.

Caleb: I thought I knew Abraham well. But this surprises me. He acted like a puppy: "Go ahead, Lot. Take what you want. Don't let me get in your way. Yes, I know I'm your elder. Yes, I know you're being blessed for my sake. But don't let that hold you back."

Lamech: I had wished better from my master too. No humility. No insight into the big picture. Only looking out for himself. Dear friend, I agree. We should separate, but there's plenty of room right here in the high country.

Caleb: Lot made a pretty good choice, didn't he? He'll find all the pastureland he needs—and more—in the Jordan Valley.

Lamech: True. But when he—and we with him—go down into that valley, I fear we're going to find more than good pasture. I hope he doesn't drag us into one of the cities. After all, Lot knows the promises God gave to Abraham. He's heard them every time Abraham built one of his altars. But he doesn't seem to listen. Why didn't he stay closer to Abraham? Why didn't he ask Abraham for advice? Why didn't he let Abraham choose first? No, he always takes the path of hard-nosed economic logic.

Caleb: I share your fear. The cities of Canaan around here frighten me. But nothing scares me as much as what's going on in Sodom and Gomorrah. How long will God put up with them?

Lamech: And that's just where we are headed. It's as if Lot doesn't care.

Caleb: I wonder how Abraham will feel when he watches you all head down there. I know he loves Lot.

Lamech: Would you pray for us? Ask God to make my master realize what he's getting into.

Caleb: Yes. I'll do that. If only Lot was meek like my master, Abraham. If he were, he would inherit the earth along with Abraham. If only he looked ahead to his eternity in Heaven. There he'll find more pastureland than he could ever imagine.

Abraham in the New Testament

Hebrews 11:9,10,13-16

As you read this New Testament description of Abraham's faith, put yourself in Abraham's shoes as he was deciding how to handle the conflict between his herdsmen and Lot's.

> [9] By faith he lived as a stranger in the Promised Land, as if it did not belong to him, dwelling in tents along with Isaac and Jacob, who were heirs with him of the same promise. [10] For he was looking forward to the city that has foundations, whose architect and builder is God. . . .
>
> [13] All of these [Old Testament believers] died in faith, without having received the things that were promised, but they saw and welcomed them from a distance. They confessed that they were strangers and pilgrims on the earth. [14] Indeed, people who say things like that make it clear that they are looking for a land of their own. [15] And if they were remembering the land they had come from, they would have had an opportunity to return. [16] Instead, they were longing for a better land—a

heavenly one. For that reason, God is not ashamed to be called their God, because he prepared a city for them. (Hebrews 11:9,10;13-16)

What we learn about Abraham from the New Testament: Abraham's first consideration was not his earthly welfare but his heavenly welfare. What happened to him on earth was temporary. What would happen in eternity would be forever. He could accept living in tents on earth because he had "a city that has foundations" awaiting him. Moreover, Abraham knew that God would bless him on earth. Abraham knew that God would do this no matter where he lived in Canaan.

The Life of Abraham

Abraham Builds Another Altar—Genesis 13:18

Abraham moved to Hebron. Hebron is about 30 miles south of Bethel, located in the mountainous land of central Canaan. There he built another altar to the Lord. In the first two chapters of Abraham's story, we count three altars he built (Genesis 12:7,8; 13:18). And we noted that he made a return visit to one of them (Genesis 13:4). This tells us about Abraham's devotion to the Lord and his appreciation of the Lord's promises. Abraham always treasured God's promise to give him the whole land of Canaan. But even more important to Abraham were the little plots of land on which he built altars and called on the name of the Lord.

The Conversation

This conversation illustrates what the servants might have discussed about God after listening to Abraham call on his name, especially after they heard Abraham distinguish the true God from the false gods of the nations around them. The characters and the conversation are hypothetical.

The characters:

Caleb: A mature believer in the true God and one of Abraham's servants.

Chloe: Caleb's wife, also a mature believer in the true God.

Abihu: A man who is somewhat skeptical about Abraham's faith.

Anna: Abihu's wife, who shares Abihu's thoughts.

Merit: One of the servants Pharaoh gave to Abraham.

> *Abihu:* I'm glad we didn't throw out our gods.
>
> *Anna:* Me too. I would rather pray to gods I can see and touch.
>
> *Merit:* Excuse me. I don't understand. What did Abraham mean by "the true God?" I know what Abihu and Anna are talking about. Our house in Egypt was next to the temple of Ra. He's the big one. But there are dozens of lesser gods. And they're not the puny little pieces of wood and stone you people keep in boxes. They're giant statues, made by the best carvers in the world. I can't imagine any god who doesn't want his statue in every park and his picture on every wall.

Caleb: Merit, that's just the point. The true God is not like the gods of Egypt, or of any other country. He is not one God among many. He is the only God there is. He doesn't have a form, like a human being or an animal. In fact, he's the one who made human beings, animals, and the whole universe. Egyptians worship the sun god, Ra. But the sun is just one part of God's creation.

Chloe: You are right, Merit. We can't see him. But we know he exists, and we worship him.

Merit: I would like to hear more about your God. But I must ask: Wasn't the true God strong enough to protect our master, Abraham, when he arrived in Egypt? Why did he lie about Sarah?

Anna: That's what I'm thinking too. Abraham built altars to God. He worshipped him, told us about his greatness, and prayed to him. But then, look at what he did.

Chloe: Anna, we've had our doubts too. Will God always protect us? Maybe Abraham is no different.

Caleb: But Abraham does trust the true God. Merit, look at how everything turned out. After all, if Abraham had trusted God perfectly, you and your family wouldn't be here, would you? Sometimes the true God works in mysterious ways.

Closing

Abraham and Lot separated. Lot took the best land. Abraham, however, let God guide and direct his life. The words of Psalm 47 were written by a descendant of King

David. But they might as well have been spoken by Abraham when God let him survey the Promised Land and travel through it.

Psalm 47

> Clap your hands, all peoples!
> Shout to God with loud songs of joy!
> For the LORD, the Most High, is to be feared,
>   a great king over all the earth.
> He subdued peoples under us,
>   and nations under our feet.
> He chose our heritage for us,
>   the pride of Jacob whom he loves. Selah
> God has gone up with a shout,
>   the LORD with the sound of a trumpet.
> Sing praises to God, sing praises!
> Sing praises to our King, sing praises!
> For God is the King of all the earth;
>   sing praises with a psalm!
> God reigns over the nations;
> God sits on his holy throne.
> The princes of the peoples gather
>   as the people of the God of Abraham.
> For the shields of the earth belong to God;
>   he is highly exalted!

Chapter 3
Genesis 14

Abraham Rescues Lot—14:1-16
Abraham Honors Melchizedek—14:17-24

Prayer: Dear heavenly Father, help me better understand the role Abraham played in God's plan of salvation. Abraham knew he was a sinner, and he looked forward to the coming Savior. Help me follow his example by keeping my eyes on Jesus as the source of my salvation and my eternal hope. Amen.

Keyword: "Righteousness"
Part Two: God's Gift to Believers

The Lord promised Adam and Eve a Savior. Since then, everything he did was the right way to fulfill that promise. And everything he does today is right—gathering his family of believers and bringing us safely to Heaven. That's the meaning of *the Lord's* righteousness.

This introduces us to the word righteousness in another sense, that is, *God's gift of righteousness* to a sinful world. The righteousness Christ gives us is not primarily the ability to do righteous things in our own lives. Rather, it is his gift to us, which he gained by his perfect life and innocent death. All who recognize they are sinners and deserve God's punishment can have this gift of righteousness simply by believing that it is theirs. Clothed in his righteousness, we are assured of a place in God's family and life with him forever.

In this and the next chapter of this book, we will examine the word "righteousness" in this sense—the righteousness God gives us as a gift. In this chapter of Genesis, we will meet a man named Melchizedek, who pictures Christ and the righteousness he won for us.

In the present chapter of this book, we will discuss God's gift of righteousness in Christ. In Chapter 4, we will see how Abraham acquired this gift of righteousness.

The Life of Abraham

Abraham Rescues Lot—14:1-16

Mesopotamia means the land between the rivers. The two rivers are the Tigris and Euphrates, which lie to the east of Canaan. This was Abraham's original home, lying about a thousand miles from where he was now living in Canaan. Four kings from Mesopotamia had conquered the five cities in the valley where Lot was living. This area, which Moses calls the Valley of Siddim, is the location of the modern Dead Sea. The cities included Sodom, where Lot lived, Gomorrah, Admah, Zeboiim, and Zoar.

The eastern kings were collecting yearly tribute from those five cities. After twelve years of paying tribute, the five cities rebelled. The following year, the four kings from Mesopotamia arrived to put down the rebellion and start collecting tribute again.

The four kings' main goal was to defeat the five kings in the Valley of Siddim. To do this, they started by conquering the surrounding Canaanite cities, who might come to the help of Sodom, Gomorrah, and the other cities.

The kings of Mesopotamia approached Canaan from the north. First, they attacked cities in northern Canaan. Then they went south and defeated cities along the east side of the Jordan River. After conquering those cities, they circled to the west and then turned back to face the five kings of the cities in the Valley of Siddim.

Their plan succeeded. After conquering the five cities, the Mesopotamians headed home with the plunder they had taken. Lot's poor choice of where to live and raise his herds was beginning to pay dividends. He was among the captives.

This was not Abraham's fight. But when the Mesopotamians took Lot, Abraham could not stand by. Abraham knew that God would always protect him. But that did not stop him from being prepared for the possibility of armed conflict. He had trained 318 of his servants to fight. Moses tells us that they were "born in his house"—men born and raised in the households of Abraham's longtime servants. Such servants are more loyal than servants who join a household later in life. Abraham could count on these servant/soldiers not to desert him in the heat of battle.

Abraham's well-trained army did not affect his trust in God. God does the training, as King David confessed: "Blessed be the LORD my Rock, who trains my hands for battle, my fingers for war" (Psalm 144:1).

Abraham could also count on the help of his friends, Mamre and his brothers, Aner and Eschol. They were likely permanent residents of Canaan, perhaps men whom God had led to faith. We don't know any more about them, but what a blessing for Abraham, who lived as a temporary resident in a foreign country, to have some of the locals as friends.

We are not told what was on Abraham's mind when he set out to save Lot. We don't know the size of the Mesopotamian army, but it was likely larger than Abraham's forces. One thing we do know is that by this time, the Mesopotamians were very battle-hardened.

But as one who trusted in the Lord, Abraham likely shared the thoughts expressed by another military leader, Joshua. When Joshua was old, he conveyed God's Word to the Israelites: "I sent the hornet before you, and it drove them out before you, as it drove out the two kings of the Amorites. It was not by your sword and not by your bow!" (Joshua 24:12). God's invisible hornets were always at work when his people went into battle. Abraham must have trusted that God's hornets were going before his little army, too.

Abraham was confident in God's promise to curse those who cursed him. Years later, King David reflected that promise when he faced the giant Goliath in battle. David taunted him: You will not kill me, but I will kill you, "and all those gathered here will know that the LORD does not save with sword and spear, for the battle belongs to the LORD, and he will deliver you into our hand" (1 Samuel 17:47). Notice that David did not say God would deliver Goliath into *my* hand, but into *our* hand. This was not David's battle, but a battle of the descendants of Abraham, whom Goliath was dishonoring. Although the rest of Israel's troops were too afraid of Goliath to help David, David still saw them as God's people who were living under the promise God made to Abraham.

Despite the size of his army, Abraham knew he would win because the outcome was in the Lord's hands.

CHAPTER 3   Genesis 14

Abraham immediately went north to Dan in pursuit of the Mesopotamians. Dan was the name of a tribe in Israel that later settled in northern Canaan. There God blessed Abraham's plan of attack and his soldiers' skill. He rescued Lot and pursued the four kings. We see God's hornets at work as the Mesopotamians fled from Abraham some 100 miles north to Damascus.

When we watch Abraham engage the five kings in battle, we see a man who had as much trust in the Lord as King David had. As King David would later write:

> No king is saved by the great size of his army.
> No hero is rescued by his great strength.
> You cannot rely on a horse to save you.
> Its great strength will not deliver you.
> Look, the eye of the LORD is on those who fear him,
> on those who wait for his mercy. (Psalm 33:16-18)

When we analyze Abraham's times of weakness, we should keep in mind Abraham's incredible bravery in his battle with the five kings.

Abraham Honors Melchizedek—14:17-24

Abraham returned to Canaan with the people and plunder that the Mesopotamians had taken from the five defeated cities. Among the people was his nephew Lot.

On his way home, Abraham passed through the city of Salem, which later became known as Jeru*salem*. As the group approached the city, two men came out to meet Abraham outside the city in the King's Valley (regarding the name, see 2 Samuel 18:18).

We can only guess why the king of Sodom was there. The king had evidently survived the battle, escaped the tar pit into which he had fallen (Genesis 14:10), and fled into the hills. Perhaps he knew that Salem was a place where he could find safety and sought refuge in the hands of the benevolent Melchizedek.

We now witness one of the most unusual events in the Old Testament. The second person to meet Abraham was Melchizedek. Moses doesn't give us a lengthy discussion of this event. But he teaches us the basics.

Melchizedek believed in the true God and his promise of a Savior. He understood that Abraham played an important role in the fulfillment of that promise. We don't know how Melchizedek came to know this. But he expressed his awareness of Abraham's greatness by meeting him with gifts of bread and wine.

Then Melchizedek praised God for protecting Abraham from his enemies—most recently by protecting him in the battle against the Mesopotamian kings: "Blessed be Abram by God Most High, Creator of heaven and earth. And blessed be God Most High, who delivered your enemies into your hand" (Genesis 14:19,20).

But Melchizedek was even greater than Abraham. He was a special king. "Melech" means king, and "Zedek" means peace. Melchizedek was king of the city of Salem. "Salem" means peace. He was also priest of "God Most High," whom Melchizedek had asked to bless Abraham. Abraham was glad to be in the presence of such a person. Moses tells us that Abraham honored Melchizedek as his superior by giving him a "tithe" (a tenth) of the plunder he had recovered.

Melchizedek is mentioned only one more time in the Old Testament. In Psalm 110, David prophesies about the coming Savior. He tells us about Jesus' power, his victory over his enemies, and his coming rule as King over the whole world. In that psalm, David also says that Jesus will be a priest, a special priest, different from the priests of the old covenant who served God in David's day. He writes, "The LORD has sworn and will not change his mind, 'You are a priest forever after the order of Melchizedek'" (Psalm 110:4). That simple statement links Melchizedek to Jesus, and it helps us understand why Abraham honored him as he did.

The king of Sodom was genuinely grateful to Abraham for saving him and his people. So, he wanted to give Abraham the goods Abraham had recovered from the Mesopotamian kings. But Abraham refused to take them. This was because God had promised to bless Abraham. Abraham wanted to give God all the glory for making him rich. He didn't want anyone to get the idea that someone else had done that in God's place.

Abraham knew that God had made this promise only to him. He did not rigidly enforce his refusing to take the money on others. He was kind to Mamre and his two other friends, who had helped him win the victory, and he allowed them to take their share of the plunder.

Abraham and Melchizedek in the New Testament

Hebrews 7:1-9,17

In Hebrews, chapters 5-7, the writer picks up on David's statement in Psalm 110 and fleshes out what Moses tells us about Melchizedek in Genesis 14. The writer explains:

> [1] This Melchizedek, king of Salem, priest of the Most High God, is the one who met Abraham as he was returning from the defeat of the kings and blessed

him, ² and Abraham gave him a tenth of everything. First, Melchizedek means "king of righteousness," and then "king of Salem," which is "king of peace." ³ He is without father or mother, without genealogy, without beginning of days or end of life, and resembling the Son of God, he remains a priest forever.

⁴ Consider how great this man was. Even Abraham, the patriarch, gave him a tenth from the best of the spoils. ⁵ According to the Law, those sons of Levi who received the priesthood have a command to collect a tenth from the people, that is, from their brother Israelites, even though they also came from Abraham's body. ⁶ But here the one who was not descended from them collected a tenth from Abraham and blessed the one who had the promises. ⁷ And without any question, it is the lesser who is blessed by the greater.

⁸ In the one case, those who are mortal collect the tenth; in the other case, the one who collects has testimony in Scripture that he lives. ⁹ And, through Abraham, even Levi, who collects the tenth, has paid a tenth, so to speak, ¹⁰ because he was still in the body of his forefather when Melchizedek met Abraham.

The book of Hebrews was primarily written to Jews who had converted to Christianity. These converts were undergoing tremendous pressure from friends and relatives to forsake Jesus and return to the Old Testament laws of Moses. To help the new Christians combat this pressure, the writer of Hebrews described the superiority of Jesus' priesthood over that of the Old Testament priests.

Jesus' priesthood provided much more than the Old Testament priests could provide. In Hebrews 6:19,20, the writer talks about the hope Christ has given us through his suffering and death: "We have this hope as an anchor for the soul. It is sure and firm, and it goes behind the inner curtain, where Jesus entered ahead of us on our behalf, because he became a high priest forever like Melchizedek." Our hope in Jesus is like an anchor that secures a boat. Jesus, our hope, ascended into Heaven and is fixed there. With hands that hold onto Jesus' gift of righteousness and his gracious forgiveness, believers are kept safe throughout their lives. Our anchor is firm and secure, and someday Christ will yank on the anchor rope and pull us up to him.

This is something the Old Testament priests could never do. Those priests could offer sacrifices for the people and pray for them. But their sacrifices could never truly remove the guilt of sin. And because they themselves were sinners, they could never be our anchor in Heaven. They all died and had to be replaced.

The writer of Hebrews takes us deeper into the difference between the Old Testament and the New Testament priesthood. The Old Testament priests all came from the family of Moses' brother Aaron and were all members of his priestly order. But because of their human imperfections, a different and better priesthood is needed—a priesthood from a different "order." Jesus was that perfect high priest; his person, gifts, and power went beyond those of the priests from the "order" of Aaron.

Jesus was a priest in a different and higher order. Melchizedek was in this order. In fact, David, the author of Psalm 110, named this order after him: "the order of Melchizedek" (verse 4, NIV84).

The writer of Hebrews repeats some of what Moses told us about Melchizedek's greatness. But he adds some details that help us better understand the greatness of the new order, of which Jesus is the high priest. Here is a summary of everything that Moses and the writer of Hebrews tell us about the ways Melchizedek and Jesus were the same.

First, Melchizedek was a "king." Like Christ, he was a powerful person, having authority to rule.

Second, he was king of Salem. Salem means "peace." So Melchizedek's royal power brought peace, like Jesus' rule does. And the city over which they rule is a peaceful city.

Third, Melchizedek was priest of the "Most High God." That became clear when Melchizedek prayed that "God Most High, Creator of heaven and earth" would bless Abraham (Genesis 14:19). And it also became clear when he thanked "God Most High" for enabling Abraham to conquer his enemies (Genesis 14:20). Jesus was the King and Priest given to us by God Most High.

Fourth, the name Melchizedek means "king of righteousness." This gets us back to the keyword of this chapter, righteousness. This word links Melchizedek to Christ. Christ did the right thing to save the world from sin: His life and death gave the gift of righteousness to the entire world. For those who know their sins, the righteousness of Christ is theirs for the taking. In other words, through faith Christ's righteousness becomes ours and enables us to live at peace with God.

Fifth, Melchizedek appeared on the pages of Scripture without a record of his parentage and then disappeared without a record of his death. This pictures Jesus. He had no human father. He was born of the Holy Spirit through the Virgin Mary. And when his time on earth was over, he disappeared into Heaven, where he now lives.

CHAPTER 3   Genesis 14

Sixth, Abraham knew that Melchizedek was greater than him. So he gave Melchizedek a tithe of the plunder he had recovered. This shows the difference in greatness between the Old Testament priests and Jesus, our priest in the order of Melchizedek. The priests in the order of Aaron, who descended from Abraham, were commanded to *take* tithes from the people of Israel to provide for their earthly needs. The priests themselves were not required to *give* tithes to anyone else. However—and this shows how great Melchizedek was—when Abraham gave a tithe to Melchizedek, it's as if the priests in the order of Aaron (the priests established by the law of Moses) were giving tithes to Melchizedek. In other words, the Old Testament priests themselves honored Melchizedek and Christ, recognizing them as greater priests than themselves.

Seventh, Melchizedek blessed Abraham. This shows that Melchizedek honored Abraham as the father of the Savior. But it also shows that Melchizedek was greater than Abraham. After all, the writer of Hebrews says, a person can only be blessed by someone greater. By accepting Melchizedek's blessing, Abraham was confessing that Melchizedek was greater than him.

Eighth, it was necessary that there be a priest like Melchizedek. The Old Testament priests were all sinners. They died and had to be replaced by other priests, who had to be replaced by still others. Only a timeless person could continue as a priest forever and for all people. That is what Jesus is—a timeless priest in the order of Melchizedek, whose service to us never ends.

The meeting between Abraham and Melchizedek was a meeting between (1) the man who fathered priests to serve the people of Israel before Christ was born and (2) a man who pictured Jesus' greater priesthood. His meeting with Melchizedek helped Abraham anticipate the time when he would be a blessing to the entire world through his great descendant, Jesus. As Jesus said, "Your father Abraham was glad that he would see my day. He saw it and rejoiced" (John 8:56).

The writer of Hebrews draws the following conclusion from this:

> [11] So if everything could have been brought to its goal through the Levitical priesthood (for the people received the law on the basis of that priesthood), what further need was there for another priest to arise who was like Melchizedek, yet not said to be like Aaron? [17] For it has been testified in Scripture about him: You are a priest forever, like Melchizedek. (Hebrews 7:11,17)

What we learn about Abraham from the New Testament: Abraham understood the greatness of Melchizedek—his kingship over the city of peace, the righteousness that characterized his kingdom, and his position as priest of a new order. He knew Melchizedek prefigured the great High Priest, whose coming he rejoiced in. We follow Abraham's example by honoring Jesus as our Savior and our King.

The Conversation

This conversation is between Hushai and Jonathan, two of Abraham's 318 servant/soldiers, who are discussing what they have just experienced. The characters and the conversation are fictional.

The characters:

CHAPTER 3 Genesis 14

Hushai: One of Abraham's servant/soldiers

Jonathan: Another of Abraham's servant/soldiers

> *Hushai:* So, Jonathan, how did you feel when we were coming up on those Mesopotamian kings?
>
> *Jonathan:* Probably how you felt. I was terrified.
>
> *Hushai:* We've been training for this. But practicing with sticks is not like facing swords.
>
> *Jonathan:* And those guys have been using their swords every day. A city here. A town there. And finally, the five cities on the plain. And they defeated them all. It was nice that we had the help of Abraham's friends. But we were still outnumbered.
>
> *Hushai:* And Abraham is hardly a military leader. How many times has he been in a battle? At least we caught them by surprise.
>
> *Jonathan:* Is Abraham out of his mind?
>
> *Hushai:* That's the question, isn't it? But when he gathers us around those altars he builds, you can see his confidence in God. He speaks about promises God has made to him. He's confident that God will protect him.
>
> *Jonathan* laughing: I still wonder if he's out of his mind. What a great army he depended on! 318 of us who've never been in a battle!
>
> *Hushai:* Or maybe he's the only one around here who's in his right mind. If we were so weak, how could we defeat those kings and chase them a hundred miles? Maybe our weakness is the key to Abraham's strength.

Jonathan: But who comes home with tired troops like us and a bunch of captives who want nothing more than to be in their homes again, and makes a stop at Salem? And that strange person who came to meet us. He seemed to know Abraham.

Hushai: The man blessed our master Abraham, and Abraham honored him by giving him a tenth of what he'd taken in battle. There was a mutual respect going on, but I don't know why. I'm going to have to think about that. Maybe Abraham will explain it to us the next time we're gathered around his altar.

Jonathan: But I'm still upset.

Hushai: Why so?

Jonathan: Look at those donkeys. Did you see the piles of silver and gold, the clothing, and the ornaments loaded on their backs? I was thinking some of that might be mine. I sure could have used it. Look at Mamre's servants and the servants of Aner and Eshcol. Their wives will be happy when they come home. I agree with the king of Sodom. He told our master to take it all. But Abraham said, No, and brought up his God again. You wonder why Abraham has anything left when he gives it away like that!

Hushai: I'm tempted to feel the same way. But who would you rather have as your master? Some Canaanite lord or Abraham. I think I'll choose Abraham.

Closing

Other than in Genesis 14 and Hebrews 5-7, Scripture mentions Melchizedek only in Psalm 110. This is a "Messianic" psalm. That is, it speaks about the Savior (the Messiah) to come. As you read Psalm 110, reflect on the comparison between Jesus and Melchizedek which the writer of Hebrews made in Hebrews chapters 6 and 7. Note how the psalm describes the Messiah's power as King and the unique nature of his priesthood. (The last verse is often interpreted as a prophecy about Jesus' final journey to the cross.)

Psalm 110

> The decree of the Lord to my lord:
> "Sit at my right hand until I make your enemies
>   a footstool under your feet."
> The Lord will stretch out your strong scepter from
>   Zion.
> Rule in the midst of your enemies.
> Your people will be willing on the day of your power.
> In majesty of holiness, from the womb of the dawn,
>   the dew of your youth will be yours.
> The Lord has sworn and will not change his mind:
> "You are a priest forever, in the manner of
>   Melchizedek."
> The Lord is at your right hand.
> He will crush kings on the day of his wrath.
> He will judge the nations.
> He will fill valleys with corpses.
> He will crush heads over the wide world.
> He will drink from a stream beside the way;
>   therefore, he will lift up his head.

Chapter 4
Genesis 15

God Credits Righteousness to Abraham—15:1-7
God Expands His Promise Regarding Canaan—15:8-21

Prayer: Dear Lord, thank you for giving me your living and powerful Word, through which the Holy Spirit is at work when I read and study it. Without your Spirit nothing is clear, but with your Spirit, I cannot help but grow in the grace of understanding your Word and taking it to heart in my life. Give me more of your Holy Spirit. As I hear about the faith of Abraham, deepen my understanding of the meaning of faith. Amen.

Keyword: "Righteousness"
Part Three: God's Gift of Righteousness to Believers

God's *righteousness* is every act he did to fulfill his promise of a Savior. That is, everything he did was the "right" thing to do and it contributed to our salvation.

God's *righteousness* also refers to his gift of righteousness given to the entire world. As our great High Priest, God's Son brought this gift into being by his perfect life and sacrificial death.

This *righteousness* is ours through faith in the fact that Jesus, our High Priest, accomplished it for all people. This is the meaning of the word righteousness as it is used here in Genesis 15, where we will hear that God credited righteousness to Abraham through faith.

The Life of Abraham

God Credits Righteousness to Abraham—15:1-7

This event took place within the first ten years of Abraham's life in Canaan.[14] Abraham was nearing 85, and Sarah was approaching seventy-five. The promise had not yet been fulfilled. God encouraged Abraham: "Do not be afraid, Abram. I am your shield, your very great reward" (Genesis 15:1). From what God says here, something was making Abraham afraid. Perhaps it was the thought that God would not fulfill his promise.

God assured Abraham that he would continue to bless him. But as encouraging as that was, Abraham objected. "O Sovereign Lord, what can you give me since I remain childless and the one who will inherit my estate is Eliezer of Damascus?" (Genesis 15:2). (It was the custom of the day that if a man didn't have a son, the trusted manager of his household would inherit his belongings.)

God assured Abraham that his heir would not be Eliezer, "but a son coming from your own body will be your heir" (Genesis 15:4). Through a child born from him, God said, Abraham's descendants would become as numerous as the stars in the sky.

---

[14] See Genesis 16:3. The events in that chapter took place after Abraham had been living in Canaan ten years."

CHAPTER 4 Genesis 15

That put an end to Abraham's doubt. This is stated in the following verse: "Abram believed the Lord," and through his faith in God's promise, "God credited it to him as righteousness" (Genesis 15:6).

What does it mean that God credited Abraham's faith as righteousness?

In chapter two of this book, we talked about God's own righteousness. Simply put, God's righteousness is the fact that he does everything right. It would have been just for God to put Adam and Eve to death when they sinned. Instead, in grace and loving kindness, God promised a Savior.

Then, *in righteousness*, he shaped the world's history down to the smallest detail so that his promise would be fulfilled. In righteousness, he guided and directed the lives of his elect so they would hear the Gospel and come to faith. Then, in righteousness, he protected their faith and shielded them from the attacks of Satan.

Then, we met Melchizedek, whose name means "king of righteousness" and who pictured Jesus, the great King of Righteousness, whose perfect life accomplished righteousness for all people.

Now in Genesis 15:6, we find out how we can enjoy this gift of righteousness won for us by Christ. Abraham was righteous because he believed God's promise of a son. For Abraham, faith in God's promise of a son also meant faith in God's promise of a Savior. This is shown by what Jesus said about Abraham: "Your father Abraham was glad that he would see my day. He saw it and rejoiced" (John 8:56). In the same way, our faith is credited as righteousness. We believe that Jesus Christ did, in fact, win righteousness for the whole world, and we know that this gift belongs to us also.

Abraham in the New Testament

Most of Paul's churches were a mix of Jews and Gentiles. By Paul's day, many Jews had left Palestine and were living in cities throughout the world. And many of the Gentiles to whom he preached had previously converted to Judaism. They would have known about Abraham and how important he was.

Paul often used Abraham to teach about the meaning of faith. Specifically, he teaches us how we should understand the words, "Abraham believed in the LORD, and the LORD credited it to him as righteousness" (Genesis 15:6).[15] Here are two examples.

Galatians 3:6-9

The Galatian Christians were being influenced by some who believed that Christians must keep the laws of Moses, especially the law of circumcision. But Christianity, Paul explained, is first and foremost a religion of faith in what God has done for us, not in what we must do for God—a religion of gifts, not of rewards. To do that, he quotes Genesis 15:6.

---

[15] The EHV translates Genesis 15:6 as "Abraham believed *in the* LORD." This is a literal translation of the Hebrew. The EHV notes, however, that the phrase can also be translated "believed the Lord" or "trusted in the LORD." These two translations make it clear that Abraham's faith was not merely belief that God exists, but faith in what God had just told him about having a son. This is what the verse is saying.

CHAPTER 4   Genesis 15

> ⁶ Abraham "believed God, and it was credited to him as righteousness." ⁷ Understand, then, that those who believe are the children of Abraham. ⁸ Foreseeing that God would justify the Gentiles by faith, Scripture proclaimed the gospel in advance to Abraham, saying, "In you, all nations will be blessed." ⁹ So then, those who have faith are blessed along with Abraham, the man of faith. (Galatians 3:6-9)

In our look at Abraham, we might be content to read about the events in Abraham's life. But it's more important to study Abraham's faith, like Paul does. His words in the above verses are essential because they tell us precisely what Abraham believed, which set the course for his life.

What did Abraham have faith in? Why did God credit his faith as righteousness? First, Abraham's faith was not a vague, general belief in God's existence. Nor was it the confidence that God would always protect him. Instead, it was faith in a very specific promise, as was the faith of all Old Testament believers. Namely, it was faith in a Savior, and that through the Savior, salvation was given as a gift to all who believed in the Savior's work.

That becomes clear from what Paul says in the above verses. Paul is saying that God's promise to bless all nations through Abraham was the Gospel message. Just as Abraham's faith was credited to him as righteousness, so righteousness would come to people from all nations through faith. Abraham knew that the Savior would come from the son God promised him. He was declared righteous through that faith. By saying that all nations would be blessed through Abraham, God was saying that Abraham was both the ancestor of the promised Savior and the model of saving faith. Abraham was doing the same thing Paul wanted his listeners to do: find their salvation through faith in Christ alone.

To be a child of Abraham means to have faith. But we must expand on that statement: To be a child of Abraham means to have the same faith Abraham had. Looking at it from the other direction, Paul carefully defined faith in all his letters. So if the children of Abraham have faith in the way Paul consistently defined it, then our father Abraham must have had the same faith. Otherwise, we would be alike only in the sense that we both have faith in *something*. But that's obviously not what Paul had in mind. We and Abraham both believe the Gospel.

The only difference between us and Abraham is the time we live in. Abraham looked ahead to the Savior and to the birth of his son through whom the Savior would be born. In the New Testament, we look back to the birth of the Savior, who came from the people descended from Abraham and his son Isaac.

Romans 4:1-5; 13-25

We'll break up this section to make it easier to follow Paul's line of thought.

Romans 4:1-5

> [1] What then will we say that Abraham, our forefather, discovered according to the flesh? [2] If indeed Abraham had been justified by works, he would have had a reason to boast—but not before God. [3] For what does Scripture say? "Abraham believed God and it was credited to him as righteousness."
>
> [4] Now to a person who works, his pay is not counted as a gift but as something owed. [5] But to the person who

does not work but believes in the God who justifies the ungodly, his faith is credited to him as righteousness.

Here, Paul made the same point he made in the verses we just quoted from Galatians. Abraham was declared righteous through faith in God's gift of a Savior from sin.[16]

Note that in this section, Paul is explaining the meaning of faith in the Gospel to New Testament Christians. However, he bases his explanation on the faith of Abraham and David. This shows that the faith of these two Old Testament men was faith in Christ and in the forgiveness of sins, just like ours is. In this way, Paul draws all believers, no matter when they lived, together in Christ.

Romans 4:13-17

> [13] Indeed, the promise that he would be the heir of the world was not given to Abraham or his descendants through the law, but through the righteousness that is by faith. [14] To be sure, if people are heirs by the law, faith is empty and the promise is nullified. [15] For law brings wrath. (Where there is no law, there is no transgression.) [16] For this reason, the promise is by faith, so that it may be according to grace and may be guaranteed to all of Abraham's descendants—not only to the one who is a descendant by law, but also to the one who has the faith of Abraham. He is the father of us all. [17] As it is written: "I have made you a father of many nations."

---

[16] "To justify" and "to declare righteous" are not two different things. They are the same. Both are translations of the same Greek word. In Romans 4:5, the Greek word used for "who justifies" is τὸν δικαιοῦντα, and the Greek for "as righteousness" is εἰς δικαιοσύνην. So, when you see the word "justify" in an English translation, realize that the translator could also have written "declare righteous."

Paul described God's promise to Abraham in a unique way. He said that Abraham would be "heir of the world." In other words, Abraham and his descendants would someday inherit this entire world and everything in it. This calls to mind what Jesus said in the third beatitude: "Blessed are the gentle [or "meek" NIV11], because they will inherit the earth" (Matthew 5:5). Since we have God's promises, we can be gentle toward those who attempt to gain worldly things by their own strength or skill. Remember how Abraham was gentle toward Lot and let him choose the best of the land. Why could he do this? Because Abraham knew the same thing that all believers know, namely, that someday the whole world would belong to him and his descendants.

Abraham received this great blessing by faith, not by keeping the law of circumcision or any of God's commandments. If Abraham had to keep the law to receive God's promises, then faith had no place in his life, and Scripture was wrong to say Abraham's faith was credited as righteousness. Deeds that go against God's Law merit God's wrath. But if we are saved by faith, the Law has no place in our receiving God's blessings. And since faith excludes the Law, our sins against the Law don't put a barrier between us and God's promises.

Since God's promises come by faith, we possess them merely because God wants to give them to us as a gift, that is, by *grace*. And for that reason, they are *guaranteed*, which could never be the case if we had to earn them.

Paul then quotes God's promise to Abraham in Genesis 17:5: "I have made you a father of many nations" (Romans 4:17). This calls to mind one of God's first promises to Abraham: "All of the families of the earth will be blessed in you" (Genesis 12:3). God gave Jewish people the Law, but the Law could never save them. They were saved by faith, just as their father Abraham was. And the Gentile nations, who could never have hoped to be saved by the Law since it was not given to them, were also included in the blessing God gave to Abraham because those blessings came by faith, and the Gentiles could certainly believe.

Romans 4:17-22

What did Abraham actually believe? He believed God's promise to him in Genesis 15:1-6:

> [17] In the presence of God, Abraham believed him who makes the dead alive and calls non-existing things so that they exist. [18] Hoping beyond what he could expect, he believed that he would become the father of many nations, just as he was told: "This is how many your descendants will be." [19] He did not weaken in faith, even though he considered his own body as good as dead (because he was about one hundred years old), and even though he considered Sarah's womb to be dead. [20] He did not waver in unbelief with respect to God's promise, but he grew strong in faith, giving glory to God [21] and being fully convinced that God was able to do what he had promised. [22] This is why "it was credited to him as righteousness." (Romans 4:17-22)

God took Abraham outside and showed him the vast number of stars in the sky (Genesis 15:5). He promised Abraham: "This is how many your descendants will be" (Romans 4:18). Abraham believed this promise even though he and Sarah were too old to have children, and humanly speaking the promise was an impossible one. This impossibility, however, didn't lead Abraham to doubt. Rather, it led him to believe the promise even more strongly and, in the process, to glorify God by confessing that he had the power to do impossible things. Because of his faith in God's promise, Abraham was considered righteous.

Romans 4:23-25

> [23] Now the statement "it was credited to him" was not written for him alone, [24] but also for us to whom it would be credited, namely, to us who believe in the one who raised our Lord Jesus from the dead. [25] He was handed over to death because of our trespasses and was raised to life because of our justification.

Not only does Paul use the New Testament to shed light on the Old Testament. The Old Testament, Paul says, sheds light on the New. The fact that Abraham was considered righteous through faith teaches us about our own righteousness through faith.

Paul joins together two impossibilities, one that Abraham believed and one that Christians believe. In both cases, they involve raising someone from the dead. Abraham believed God's "impossible" promise that he and Sarah would be raised from the dead to bear a son through whom the whole world would be blessed. We believe the "impossible" fact that God raised his son to life, whose death for sin resulted in the entire world being blessed with the forgiveness of sins. Faith that God accomplished these impossible things is credited as righteousness.

Was all this as clear to Abraham as it was to Paul? Yes. God's promise to Adam and Eve centered on a child who would be born from a woman—a person who would bless the whole world by crushing the Serpent's head. God had promised Abraham that he would be a blessing to all nations. Abraham could have interpreted this in only one way, namely, that the Savior promised to Eve would come from his line.

CHAPTER 4 Genesis 15

What we learn about Abraham from the New Testament:
When Paul explains the heart of the Christian faith, he uses Abraham as his teaching tool. The most important thing we can learn from Abraham is how we are saved. We in the New Testament can turn to Old Testament Abraham to find the heart of the Christian religion: salvation through faith in God's promised Savior without the need to earn it.

The Life of Abraham

God Expands His Promise Regarding Canaan—15:8-21

These verses turn our attention from God's promise that Abraham would have a son to his promise that Abraham's descendants would inherit the land of Canaan. The promise of a son was meant for all people. The promise of the land of Canaan was given only to Abraham's descendants and was part of the way God would safeguard the message of the Gospel and create the place where the Savior would be born.

After God assured Abraham that he would have a son, he assured Abraham that he would someday possess the land of Canaan. Abraham asked, "LORD God, how will I know that I will possess it?" (Genesis 15:8). What happens next is just as mysterious and amazing as Abraham's meeting with Melchizedek.

God told Abraham to prepare for a covenant ceremony—a ceremony that in the ancient world bound two parties to an agreement. We have similar "ceremonies" today. A lawyer draws up a document specifying what each party has agreed to do for the other party. At the bottom of the document are two lines, one for each party to sign. The parties sign and date the document. Sometimes, a notary is called in to verify the identity of the two parties and attest to the validity of their signatures. The document becomes legal, and it can be used in a court of law if either of the two parties fails to do what they agreed to.

In the ancient world, a ceremony sometimes replaced a legal document. The parties would take some animals, cut them in half, and line up the halves side by side with a path between them. The two parties would state the terms of their agreement and then walk together on the path between the animals. Note that the phrase translated "to make a covenant," in Hebrew, is literally "to cut a covenant." This likely refers to the cutting of the animals.

God had Abraham take three three-year-old animals, cut them in half, and then place the halves opposite each other. In addition, Abraham was to add two birds and place them opposite each other. Then Abraham waited.

While he waited, Abraham drove away the birds of prey that wanted to feed on the dead animals. These birds likely symbolized all the Satanic forces that try to undermine God's promises in Christ.

At sunset, Abraham fell into a deep sleep and was engulfed in terrifying darkness. He would fulfill his promise to Abraham's descendants, but there would be difficult times ahead. God gave the details. Abraham and his descendants would not possess the land of Canaan immediately. It would be some 400 years before that happened. In the meantime, Abraham would live in peace and die as an old man. But his descendants would be forced to live in a foreign nation where they would be afflicted. At the right time, God would punish that nation and deliver his people. The tables would be turned. Abraham's descendants would leave that nation as very wealthy people. Then they would conquer the land of Canaan and possess it as God had promised.

God gave the reason for his delay. The inhabitants of Canaan were sinners. They worshipped idols, and as we will see in the account of Sodom and Gomorrah (Genesis 18 and 19), many of them engaged in sexual sins. God wanted them to repent, and he wanted to give them more time to do so. That's what God meant when he said, "because the guilt of the Amorites [a general term for all the inhabitants of Canaan] is not yet full" (Genesis 15:16). But they refused to repent, and God's patience would come to an end. When God told the Israelites to destroy the Canaanites completely, they would be serving as his tool to punish the Canaanites for their sin and unrepentance.

Then, suddenly, "a smoking oven and a flaming torch passed between the pieces" (Genesis 15:17). God then affirmed his promise to give Abraham the land of Canaan. In fact, God expanded on his earlier promise and gave Abraham a list of the nations his descendants would someday dispossess:

> To your descendants I have given this land from the river of Egypt to the great river, the river Euphrates. I will give you the territory of the Kenites, the Kenizzites, the Kadmonites, the Hittites, the Perizzites, the Rephaites, the Amorites, the Canaanites, the Girgashites, and the Jebusites." (Genesis 15:18-21)

This ceremony was God's answer to Abraham's question of how he could be certain that he would inherit the land of Canaan. At this point, you would expect God to join Abraham and walk with him through the animals. But he didn't. God alone, symbolized by a smoking oven (a firepot) and a blazing torch, walked between the animals. This covenant was not two-sided. It was one-sided. God was visibly reaffirming his *promise* to Abraham to give him the land of Canaan.

The Conversation

The promises in Genesis 15 about Abraham's descendants were likely repeated many times by the Israelites to bolster their faith and to let them know what to watch for in the future.

We listen in on a conversation based on what we just learned. The conversation is hypothetical, but in this case, the characters are real. It takes place shortly after Jacob took his family to Egypt.

The characters:

Joseph: A great-grandson of Abraham, who became the second most powerful ruler in Egypt.

Benjamin: Another great-grandson of Abraham and Joseph's brother.

> *Benjamin:* You should have seen our father when God told him it was OK to leave Canaan and take us to Egypt.
>
> *Joseph:* I can imagine. Our family has lived in Canaan for over a hundred years. We've lived there like a bunch of strangers. We have no deeds to any property there, only God's promise that he will give it to us someday.
>
> *Benjamin:* And we had to leave Canaan. It was like giving up our grasp on the land God promised to us, as weak as that grasp was.
>
> *Joseph:* But at that point you knew God had brought me here, right?

Benjamin: Yes we did. But our father was still nervous about leaving the Promised Land. That is, until God told him it was OK. We were reluctant to leave Canaan, but our father told us what God had said to him, "I am God, the God of your father. Do not be afraid to go down to Egypt, for there I will make you into a great nation. I will go down to Egypt with you, and I will certainly bring you back again. And Joseph's hand will close your eyes" (Genesis 46:3,4).

Joseph: It's all coming true—what God told our father Abraham, that is.

Benjamin: We often talked about it at home. I can just hear our father repeating the words God spoke to Abraham on that mysterious night: "Know this! Your descendants will live as aliens in a land that is not theirs.... Afterward, your descendants will come out with great wealth" (Genesis 15:14). It has become clear. Egypt is the land God was talking about.

Joseph: But our family still needed an open door to come here. I'm still amazed at how God did that—by sending me to Egypt first and preparing Pharaoh to receive you. And here you are. A bunch of shepherds—and the Egyptians don't like shepherds—living on prime real estate. And under Pharaoh's protection.

Benjamin: What a wonderful place to live and grow. I'm sure Abraham often wondered how God would make his descendants as numerous as the stars in the sky. That would have been hard if we had remained in Canaan. But now, look at where God put us.

Joseph: And with a member of Abraham's family as a ruler in the foreign country where God would take them!

Benjamin: But when I hear God's prophecy to Abraham, some things frighten me! Sure, we've got it good now. We're protected and we'll grow. But there are dark times ahead. I don't know when, but someday the Egyptians will turn on us. They'll afflict us, and we will be their slaves.

Joseph: I think about that too. And I feel bad. But then I look at the miracles God did to get us here. And I ask myself, who's to say he won't do more miracles to get us out? It's not like we'll be running away like a bunch of scared slaves with nothing in our packs. We'll become wealthy. But I wonder how.

Benjamin: And the Egyptians will feel God's wrath for oppressing us. I admit, I'm just as clueless about how that will happen as Abraham must have been.

Joseph: God's promises are not always fulfilled right away. Nor will we always be spared difficulty and hardship. We must wait—usually in ignorance, with nothing in our hands but his promises. But that's enough. Believe me, I know!

Benjamin: So we simply believe the promises God made to Abraham. And we live with the good news that we are righteous by faith. I would rather be sure of that than know all the details of how God will shape our future.

Joseph: That's what Abraham did. I think that's the main thing we should learn from him.

Closing

Through faith in Christ, we too are heirs of God's promises to Abraham. For that reason, God continues to work wonders on our behalf.

1 Chronicles 16:8-18

> Oh give thanks to the Lord;
> > call upon his name;
> > make known his deeds among the peoples!
>
> Sing to him,
> > sing praises to him;
> > tell of all his wondrous works!
>
> Glory in his holy name;
> > let the hearts of those who seek the Lord rejoice!
>
> Seek the Lord and his strength;
> > seek his presence continually!
>
> Remember the wondrous works that he has done,
> > his miracles and the judgments he uttered,
> > O offspring of Israel his servant, children of Jacob,
> > his chosen ones!
>
> He is the Lord our God;
> > his judgments are in all the earth.
>
> Remember his covenant forever,
> > the word that he commanded for a thousand generations,
>
> the covenant that he made with Abraham,
> > his sworn promise to Isaac,
> > which he confirmed to Jacob as a statute,
> > to Israel as an everlasting covenant,
>
> saying, "To you I will give the land of Canaan,
> > as your portion for an inheritance."

Chapter 5
Genesis 16,17

The Birth of Ishmael—Chapter 16
The Covenant of Circumcision—Chapter 17

Prayer: Dear Lord, help me see what happens when I take matters into my own hands—when I try to make your promises come true through my own skill and planning. Enable me to rely on your promises in all areas of my life. More and more, help me to walk before you and be blameless, trusting in you and following your will as Abraham did. Amen.

The Life of Abraham

Ishmael Is Born—Chapter 16

It had been ten years since Abraham had settled in Canaan. He was eighty-five and Sarah was seventy-five. For ten years, the couple had been living with God's promise, but Sarah still did not have a son.

In the previous chapter, Abraham assumed that his household manager would inherit his estate. That was the custom of the day. But God promised Abraham: "One who will come out of your own body will be your heir" (Genesis 15:4).

From what we know, God had not yet said that Sarah would be the child's mother. So Sarah decided to give her servant,

Hagar, to Abraham. As long as Abraham was the father, it seemed that God's plan would allow for another woman to be the mother of the promised child. A son born to Hagar would become Sarah's son, and Sarah would build up her family through him. This too was the custom of the day. Abraham agreed.

But they did sin. Their sin was to use their own ingenuity to help God fulfill his promise. When we stray from God's promises and rely on our own reason to chart our course in life, things often go badly. We saw this with Lot, who chose what he thought was the best place to live and suffered for it.

When Hagar became pregnant, Abraham's household was thrown into turmoil. Hagar changed from Sarah's humble servant to Sarah's overlord. She looked down on Sarah and mocked her because she was barren. In retaliation, Sarah made life difficult for Hagar. Sarah also turned on Abraham and wrongly blamed him for causing this to happen. Things got so bad that Sarah asked Abraham for permission to get rid of Hagar and her son. Abraham let her do that.

So Hagar fled into the desert on the road going south to Egypt, where God met her at a well.[17] He told her to put away her pride, return to Sarah, and humbly serve her as she had done before.

God then gave Hagar a promise. Recall the promise God made to Abraham in chapter 15:5: "Now look toward the sky and count the stars, if you are able to count them. This is what your descendants will be like." This promise would overflow into Hagar's life. Her son Ishmael would not be the son God had promised Abraham, but he, too, would become

---

[17] The "Angel of the LORD" is not a created angel. He is the LORD himself. These verses make that especially clear.

a large nation. God also foretold that it would be a tough nation, living at odds with the nations around it, stirring up hostility and conflict. Ishmael became the father of the Arab peoples.

Hagar must have felt alone and abandoned by God as she sat by the well in the desert. But God told her to name her son Ishmael, a name that sounds like the Hebrew for "God heard." Hagar was a believer. When she heard this promise, she gave the well a special name: Be'er Lahai Roi, which means "well of the one who lives and sees me." She realized that God had not abandoned her. He had been watching her all along.

Hagar obeyed the Lord. She returned to Abraham and Sarah and had her son. Abraham gave him the name Ishmael, the name God had revealed to Hagar.

Keyword: "Covenant" [18]

The word "covenant" is used throughout Scripture. Understanding this word goes a long way toward understanding God, and it plays a big role in understanding the life of Abraham.

The word "covenant" is not a common word today, except in certain legal contexts. For example, when people move into a community, they are sometimes required to agree to the community's *covenant regulations*. The manager of the community agrees to care for the public spaces—streets, parks, entrances—and the homeowners agree to care for their property—mow the grass, hide the clutter, keep unused vehicles

---

[18] The Hebrew word for covenant is בְּרִית. It is pronounced bu-REETH. The "u" is short.

off the street, etc. A more common word is "contract," which means the same as covenant. For example, when a builder takes on a project, he must sign a contract to do the work for a certain amount of money. Both of these are two-way covenants. Each party agrees to perform a task for the other party.

But there is another kind of covenant, a one-way covenant. This kind of covenant is better called a promise. One party promises to do something for the other party. The other party is not required to do anything in return.

This was the first kind of covenant God made with the world. Adam and Eve sinned against the one command God had given them. Their sin carried the sentence of death. Ever since, death and suffering have filled this world. Eternal death in Hell is the punishment all people can expect on account of their sins.

But God did not let mankind remain in that horrible condition. He made a covenant with Adam and Eve and with us, their descendants. He *promised* to send a Savior, whose death on behalf of all people would restore their relationship with God.

This promise covenant is closely related to the two other keywords we've looked at in the previous chapters. It is at the heart of the meaning of God's name, "the LORD." The LORD refers to God's faithfulness in fulfilling his promise of a Savior. It is also at the heart of God's "righteousness." Everything God does is the right thing to do for the promise covenant to be fulfilled.

We could have started our list of keywords with the word covenant and then seen its relation to the other two keywords. But we have saved covenant until now because in

Genesis 17 God gave Abraham and his descendants a second covenant, the covenant of circumcision. This was a regular two-way covenant, where each party had to do something for the other.

At this point, we need to sort out these two covenants and keep them separate in our minds. As we said above, the word "covenant" can refer either to a promise or to a two-way agreement. The *promise* of a Savior was given to Adam and Eve. God repeated this promise to Abraham in Genesis 12:3, "All of the families of the earth will be blessed in you." At first, this was the only covenant Abraham had to think about.

But in Genesis 17, God gave Abraham another covenant, a *two-way covenant*. This was the covenant of circumcision. A person became a member of God's people on the condition that he be circumcised.

God was about to make Abraham into the great nation he had promised. This Law set Abraham and his descendants apart from the idol-worshipping nations around them. Circumcision was a sign of the righteousness Abraham had by faith.

The covenant of circumcision was the only law God gave to Abraham, Isaac, Jacob, and their family until they grew into a large nation in Egypt, and until they left there as God promised they would. But after the Israelites left Egypt, God knew that for various reasons, they needed more laws. So he gave Israel a vastly expanded Law covenant. He impressed on them the moral Law by giving them the Ten Commandments from Mount Sinai in a display of power. He then gave them laws that would define how they were to worship him and how they were to carry out their day-to-day lives.

It is easy to see how God's love was on display when he gave the promise covenant of a Savior. It is harder to see his love when he gave the two-way covenant of circumcision, and especially later when he gave his many laws through Moses.

But the Law covenant with its many requirements did several things. It marked Abraham's descendants as a nation whose God was wise and just. This would attract others to Israel to learn about the true God.

By keeping their side of the law covenant, the Israelites would glorify God. God in turn would put his glory on display by blessing them with protection, riches, and a special land in which to live. In the process, non-Israelites would believe that he was the true God and come to faith in him.

There was also another purpose. Paul wrote, "Then what about the law? It was added for the purpose of revealing transgressions until the Seed to whom the promise referred had come" (Galatians 3:19). The Law was meant to impress on the people that they were sinners and could never keep his laws perfectly. In fact, the Law actually stirred up their sinful nature to commit more sins, which further impressed on them how much they needed God's mercy.

But many of the Laws did more. In many ways, God's two-way Law covenant pointed the people to his one-way covenant promise of a Savior, which was always in effect. Many of the laws showed them how they could be free from the guilt of their sins. For example, the many sacrifices prescribed in Moses' Law pointed the people ahead to the great sacrifice the Savior would make for them. Festivals like the Passover and the Great Day of Atonement taught the people about God's mercy through the coming Savior. There were also washings and cleansing rites to observe. The Jewish people were commanded to keep these laws, but in the very act of keeping them, they were pointed to the Savior through whom they could find true cleansing from sin. In this respect, the laws served as "a shadow of the things that were coming," namely, Christ (Colossians 2:17).

Christ's suffering and death put an end to the two-way, Law covenant. Jesus said, "Do not think that I came to destroy the Law or the Prophets. I did not come to destroy them but to fulfill them" (Matthew 5:7). Once that was accomplished, the Law covenant was no longer needed; it had accomplished its purpose.

In the early church, some insisted that to be a Christian, both Jews and Gentiles had to be circumcised and obey the laws of Moses. In the book of Acts, Luke tells us, "Some men came down from Judea and began to teach the brothers: 'Unless you are circumcised according to the Law handed down by Moses, you cannot be saved'" (Acts 15:1). Were they right? This question caused the New Testament church to seek the Holy Spirit's guidance. After discussing the matter, the church leaders answered, No. They responded to those who wanted Christians to obey the Law: "Now then, why are you testing God by putting on the necks of the disciples a yoke, which neither our fathers nor we have been able to bear? On the contrary! We believe that we are saved in the same way they [the Gentiles] are—through the grace of our Lord Jesus" (Acts 15:10-11). Paul could write, "Therefore, do not let anyone judge you in regard to food or drink, or in regard to a festival or a New Moon or a Sabbath day. These are a shadow of the things that were coming, but the body belongs to Christ" (Colossians 2:16-17).

We can sort out the matter like this. In the world's history, there are two periods when there was only a single covenant: the promise of a Savior from sin. The first period began when God gave Adam and Eve the unconditional promise of a Savior. Up until Genesis 17, when God gave Abraham the two-way covenant of circumcision, that was the only covenant that existed. The second period when there was only one covenant—again, the one-way covenant promised—began after Jesus fulfilled the Law and died for the world's sins. This period will continue until Judgment Day.

But after God gave Abraham the covenant of circumcision, and after God gave his many laws through Moses, a second covenant was in place. This was a two-way Law covenant, which Israel was required to keep.

But here is the important point: As we will hear Paul say, during the years the two-way Law covenant was in effect, the one-way promise covenant was also in effect. God's promise of a Savior was always there, providing peace and hope to all who sinned against the two-way covenant. These two covenants, which were actually the opposite of each other, existed side by side throughout the history of Israel before the coming of Christ. They were opposite, but they were related: When the Israelites sinned against the Law covenant, which they invariably did, they were forced to find their hope in the promise of a Savior. What is more, many of the things *Israel had to do for God* under the Law covenant pictured *what God would do for them* when he finally fulfilled his promise—his one-way covenant of a Savior. These were the sacrifices, the special festival laws, and the laws of purification that we referred to above. When they kept these laws, they came face to face with God's mercy and forgiveness.

In summary, God introduced the Law covenant (1) for a set time, (2) for a specific group of people, and (3) for specific but temporary purposes. It never replaced the promise God gave to Adam and Eve, which applied to them and to the rest of the world. Instead, the Law was given to help the Israelites realize their need for the promise and to think about it every day.

But then, Jesus, the promised Savior and God's Son, came to earth and fulfilled the Law. At the last Passover meal he would eat with his disciples:

> He took bread, and when he had given thanks, he broke it and gave it to them, saying, "This is my body, which is given for you. Do this in remembrance of me." In the same way, he took the cup after the supper, saying, "This cup is the *new testament* [that is, the *new covenant*] *in my blood*, which is being poured out for you." (Luke 22:19-20)

Jesus called God's promise of forgiveness through him a new covenant. But it was new only because it followed the old Law covenant and fulfilled it. It was really the first covenant, the oldest of the two covenants, given long before the Law covenant was given.

In a striking way, the writer of Hebrews described the change that took place when Jesus fulfilled the Law covenant. He characterized the Law covenant by what happened when God spoke the Ten Commandments from Mount Sinai:

> You have not come to a mountain that can be touched and to burning fire, to darkness, to gloom, to a raging storm, to the sound of a trumpet, and to a voice that spoke. Those who heard the voice asked that not one more word be added, because they could not endure what was commanded: "If even an animal touches the

mountain, it must be stoned." The sight was so terrifying that even Moses said, "I am trembling with fear." (Hebrews 12:18-21)

By way of contrast, the "mountain" before which we now stand in Christ has an entirely different appearance:

You have come to Mount Zion, the city of the living God; to the heavenly Jerusalem; to tens of thousands of angels in joyful assembly; to the church of the firstborn whose names are written in heaven; to God, who is the judge of all; to the spirits of righteous people who have been made perfect; to Jesus, the mediator of a new testament; and to the sprinkled blood that speaks a better message than the blood of Abel. (Hebrews 12:22-24)

Whether a believer lived in Abraham's day, in the days when the Mosaic Law was in effect, or in the days after Jesus death and resurrection, that person is alive on Mount Zion, the heavenly Jerusalem.

The Life of Abraham

God Initiates Circumcision—Chapter 17

Chapter 17 marks an important point in Abraham's life. Thirteen years had passed since Hagar gave birth to Ishmael. Abraham was now ninety-nine, and Sarah was eighty-nine.

Abraham was still under the impression that Ishmael was the promised son. But that was about to change. God was now ready to give Abraham the child he had promised. So, he introduced some changes into Abraham's life: he changed the names of Abraham and Sarah, gave Abraham and his descendants the rite of circumcision, and made it clear that Ishmael was not the promised son.

CHAPTER 5   Genesis 16,17

First, God changed Abraham's and Sarah's names. God changed Abram (his name up to this point) to Abraham. God also changed Sarai's name to Sarah. The names do not have widely different meanings. The EHV contains the following notes: "Abram and Abraham are variants of the same name. Both mean exalted father, but Abraham sounds more like the Hebrew for father of a multitude. . . . Sarai and Sarah are variants of the same name. Both mean princess."[19] The significance of the name changes was that they signaled the great change that was about to take place in their lives. The door would be open for Abraham to become the father of many nations through the son born to him. Sarah was to become royalty, surrounded by the kings of the nations who would someday come from her.

Second, for the first time, Scripture tells us, the readers, that Sarah would be the mother of the promised child. The child's name was to be Isaac, which means "laughter." When Abraham heard God's promise that he and Sarah would have a son, he laughed with joy (Genesis 17:17). But he still wrestled with the same doubt that had led him and Sarah to have a son by Hagar. So he asked God to make Ishmael the son of the promise. But God said, No. Sarah would bear the promised son. And about that son God said, "I will establish my covenant with him as an everlasting covenant for his descendants after him" (Genesis 17:19).

Third, God gave Abraham the covenant of circumcision. The act of circumcising a male baby (cutting off his foreskin) had been practiced in ancient and modern times, most often for hygienic reasons. For Abraham and his descendants, however, it would be a religious ceremony that would separate

---

[19] See the Evangelical Heritage Version notes on Genesis 17:5,15.

Abraham's physical descendants and his household from the nations around them.

The covenant of circumcision was a Law covenant. This was the first among the many special laws that God would later give to Israel through Moses. In the promise God made with Abraham—that he would bless all nations through him—there was no hint that its fulfillment was conditioned on Abraham's response. But the covenant of circumcision was a two-way agreement. Abraham and his descendants would be blessed if they circumcised themselves. Anyone who was not circumcised "must be cut off from his people. He has broken my covenant" (Genesis 17:14).

On the very day God gave Abraham the command, Abraham carried it out: "On the same day, both Abraham and Ishmael, his son, were circumcised. All the men of his house, those born in the house as well as those purchased with money from a foreigner, were circumcised along with him" (Genesis 17:26,27).

Abraham in the New Testament

For hundreds of years, Jewish males had to be circumcised. For this reason, it was natural that questions about circumcision arose in the early church. The New Testament writers explained the relationship between Abraham's faith and his circumcision.

John 7:22

God's covenant of circumcision to Abraham was folded into the Mosaic Law.

> Moses has given you circumcision (not that it comes from Moses, but from the fathers). (John 7:22)

For a long time, there was only one law in the two-way covenant God gave to Abraham's descendants, the law of circumcision. But later, when God was delivering the Israelites from Egypt and leading the nation of Israel to the land he had promised to give them, he had them stop for a year in the desert next to a mountain called Sinai. There, he gave them a whole set of laws to teach them how to live as his people and to separate them from the idolatrous nations around them. (Jesus explained that circumcision was part of the Mosaic Law even though it actually originated with Abraham, Isaac, and Jacob.)

Acts 15:8-11

During the years before Abraham was circumcised, he was righteous through faith.

In the New Testament church, was it necessary to circumcise new believers? A council was held in Jerusalem to answer that question. As we saw previously, under the direction of the Holy Spirit the leaders of the early church said, no. They concluded that the laws of Moses were only meant for the Israelites and only until God fulfilled his promise to send a Savior.

The church answered the question at a council in Jerusalem, described in Acts 15. There, Peter brought up his experience of watching God pour out the Holy Spirit on uncircumcised Gentiles in the home of Cornelius, a Roman centurion. Peter explained what God was teaching him through this:

> [8] God, who knows the heart, testified on their behalf by giving them the Holy Spirit, exactly as he gave him to us. [9] He also showed that there is no distinction between us and them, cleansing their hearts by faith. Now then, why are you testing God by putting on the necks

of the disciples a yoke, which neither our fathers nor we have been able to bear? On the contrary! We believe that we are saved in the same way they are—through the grace of our Lord Jesus. (Acts 15:8-11)

In Romans 4, Paul used the timing of two events in Abraham's life, namely, when God credited Abraham's faith for righteousness (the Gospel), and when God gave Abraham the covenant of circumcision (a law).

Romans 4:9-11

In Romans 4, Paul used the time relation between two events in Abraham's life to explain the meaning of circumcision, namely, when God credited Abraham's faith for righteousness (the Gospel) and when God gave Abraham the covenant of circumcision (a law).

> [9] Now then, does this blessing apply only to the circumcised or also to the uncircumcised? To be sure, we maintain that faith was credited to Abraham as righteousness. [10] So then, under what circumstances was it credited to him? Was he circumcised or uncircumcised at that time? He was not circumcised but uncircumcised, [11] and he received the mark of circumcision as the seal of the righteousness by faith that was already his while he was uncircumcised.

The events of Genesis 15 (where God credited righteousness to Abraham through faith in his Gospel promise) took place about 15 years before the events of Genesis 17 (where God gave Abraham the Law covenant of circumcision).

Therefore, at the time when Abraham's faith was credited as righteousness, there was nothing to distinguish him from all the other people in the world. Along with every other male, he was uncircumcised. But later, when God gave Abraham the covenant of circumcision, he created a division between Abraham's descendants and the people of other nations.[20]

If we understand it correctly, we might say that Abraham was still a Gentile when he was declared righteous. And we might say that he first became a Jew some 15 years later when he received the covenant of circumcision, which set Jews and Gentiles apart.

God intended circumcision to point out something special about Abraham and his descendants. In Romans 4:11, Paul said that circumcision was a "mark" of faith, a "seal" of the righteousness that comes through faith.[21] It marked Abraham and his descendants as people who were righteous, not because they kept the covenant of circumcision, but because they had faith that God would send a Savior. In a sense, circumcision was separation for the purpose of evangelism. It was a mark that could lead to a discussion of how a person can become righteous before God, which would lead to a discussion about the coming Savior.

Galatians 3:13-18

The laws God gave to Abraham and his descendants did not replace the Gospel promise.

---

[20] In Romans 9:4,5 Paul described what set the Jews apart from the Gentiles: "Theirs are the adoption as sons, the glory, the covenants, the giving of the Law, the worship, and the promises. Theirs are the patriarchs, and from them, according to the flesh, came the Christ, who is God over all, eternally blessed."

[21] In English, the word "seal" can be used for an object that actually does something. For example, "the zoo keepers put a seal on the cage so that the lions couldn't escape." But the Greek word used in this verse refers to an official mark of authenticity or a certificate that verifies something as genuine. Circumcision did not make Abraham's righteousness more certain. Rather, it was a sign that Abraham was already righteous by faith.

What happened to the promise covenant when the Law covenant went into effect? Paul explains:

> [13] Christ redeemed us from the curse of the law by becoming a curse for us. As it is written, "Cursed is everyone who hangs on a tree."[14] He redeemed us in order that the blessing of Abraham would come to the Gentiles through Christ Jesus, so that we would receive the promised Spirit through faith.
>
> [15] Brothers, I am speaking in human terms. When someone has established a last will and testament, no one nullifies it or adds to it. [16] The promises God spoke referred to Abraham and to his seed. It doesn't say, "And to seeds," as if it were referring to many, but, as referring to one, "And to your seed," who is Christ. [17] What I am saying is this: The law, which came into being 430 years after the covenant established earlier by God in Christ, does not annul that covenant, with the result that it invalidates the promise. [18] In fact, if the inheritance is by the law, it is no longer by the promise. But God graciously gave it to Abraham by a promise.

We speak about the *Old Testament*, which covers the period when Israel was under the Law, and the *New Testament*, which covers the period after Jesus was born. When a person is asked, "Which came first, the old covenant or the new covenant?" the knee-jerk reaction is to answer, "The old covenant. After all, old things always come before new things."

But Paul reverses our thinking. God gave Gospel promises to Abraham, which are summarized in Genesis 12:2,3. Then, some 430 years later, God gave the Law through Moses. There was an important purpose for the Law, but regardless of how important that purpose was, it did not replace or substitute for the Gospel promise.

Paul then returns to his main point, namely, that salvation through the Law and salvation through the Gospel promise are opposites. It was a gracious gift to Abraham, as it is to all people. No one can keep God's laws. But everyone can believe that Christ fulfilled the Law and removed its demands. That included the people in Abraham's day, the people in Moses' day, and the people in the days after Christ. That's why it was so important to realize that "seed" was not a collective, referring to the Israelite nation, but a singular, referring to the one descendant of Abraham. Abraham would be a blessing to the world, but not through the Israelite people who were bound under Moses' laws. He would be a blessing to the world because he was the ancestor of Christ, through whom God freed the world from sin and death.

Romans 2:25-29; Romans 4:11,12,16

A Jew's physical circumcision is always to be accompanied by circumcision of the heart.

Many Jews in Paul's day considered themselves to be people of God on account of their descent from Abraham and their physical circumcision. Paul explained that outward, physical circumcision did not make a person truly circumcised. But true circumcision of the heart did. He wrote:

> 2:25 Indeed, circumcision has value if you observe the law. On the other hand, if you are a lawbreaker, your circumcision has become uncircumcision. 26 So, if an uncircumcised person keeps the righteous requirements of the law, won't his uncircumcision be credited to him as circumcision? 27 The one who is not circumcised physically, but who fulfills the law, will judge you who are a lawbreaker, even though you have the written law and circumcision. 28 A Jew who is merely one outwardly is not really a Jew, and circumcision that is only

outward in the flesh is not really circumcision. [29] Rather, a real Jew is one on the inside, and his circumcision is of the heart—a spiritual circumcision, not one based on carrying out the letter of the law. (Romans 2:25-29)

[4:11] So Abraham is the father of all the uncircumcised people who believe, so that righteousness would also be credited to them. [12] He is also the father of the circumcised people who are not merely circumcised but also walk in the footsteps of the faith our father Abraham had before he was circumcised.... [16] He is the father of us all. (Romans 4:11,12,16)

It was always this way. Abraham's physical circumcision was a mark of the righteousness he had by faith. And the righteousness Abraham had by faith led to a life of service to God.

The Old Testament writers warned the Jewish people against relying on mere physical circumcision. Their physical circumcision was to serve as a sign of the righteousness they had by faith in God's promise.

As with Abraham, their faith should have created love for God, through whom they had been declared righteous. They were to put away the idols they often worshipped and the sins they refused to give up. Moses urged them: "So cut away the tough shell of your sinful nature, and do not be stubborn any longer" (Deuteronomy 10:16).

The prophet Jeremiah urged the people of Judah to do the same. Otherwise, the Lord would pour out his anger on them. He wrote:

> Circumcise yourselves to the LORD. Circumcise your hearts, you men of Judah, you who live in Jerusalem. Otherwise, my rage will burn like fire, fire that can-

not be put out, because of the evil that you have done. (Jeremiah 4:4)

Moses knew that the Israelites would continue to resist God and incur his anger. He also knew that God would punish them by deporting them to foreign lands. But they should never lose hope. If they repented, returned to the faith of their father Abraham, and followed the Lord's will, he would bring them back to the land of Canaan. And he himself would circumcise their hearts so they could love the LORD:

> The LORD your God will circumcise your hearts and the hearts of your descendants, so that you love the LORD your God with all your heart and with all your soul, with the result that you will live. (Deuteronomy 30:6)

Physical circumcision was easy to do. But faith in the coming Savior and circumcision of the heart were gifts of God, which God wanted so much to give his Old Testament people.

Matthew 3:7-9

Those whose life reflected the righteousness they have by faith were true children of Abraham. The New Testament often speaks this way.

> ⁷ But when he saw many of the Pharisees and Sadducees coming for his baptism, he said to them, "You offspring of vipers, who warned you to flee from the coming wrath? ⁸ Therefore produce fruit in keeping with repentance! ⁹ Do not think of saying to yourselves, 'We have Abraham as our father.' For I tell you that God is able to raise up children for Abraham from these stones."

John the Baptist worked to prepare the Jewish people for the arrival of the promised Savior. But he was confronted by the Pharisees of his day. He warned them against thinking they were children of Abraham. They lacked the fruit of repentance, which Abraham had and put on display in his life.

Luke 13:16

> [16] Here is this daughter of Abraham, whom Satan has bound for eighteen years! Shouldn't she be set free from this bondage on the Sabbath day?"

Jesus was calling a woman he had healed a "daughter of Abraham." She was descended from Abraham, but more importantly, she shared Abraham's faith in Christ.

1 Peter 3:6

> [6] Sarah obeyed Abraham and called him lord. You are her daughters if you do what is good and do not fear anything that is intimidating.

Peter describes the fruit of Sarah's faith. Bearing such fruit makes a woman a daughter of Sarah and Abraham.

Luke 19:9

> [9] Jesus said to him, "Today, salvation has come to this house, because he too is a son of Abraham."

The tax collector, Zacchaeus, was intent on seeing Jesus when he passed by. Jesus called him a son of Abraham, as evidenced by his desire to see Jesus, to give up his corrupt ways, and to restore everything he had stolen.

John 8:31-40

³¹ So Jesus said to the Jews who had believed him, "If you remain in my word, you are really my disciples. ³² You will also know the truth, and the truth will set you free."

³³ "We are Abraham's descendants," they answered, "and we have never been slaves of anyone. How can you say, 'You will be set free'?"

³⁴ Jesus answered, "Amen, Amen, I tell you: Everyone who keeps committing sin is a slave to sin. ³⁵ But a slave does not remain in the family forever. A son does remain forever. ³⁶ So if the Son sets you free, you really will be free. ³⁷ I know you are Abraham's descendants. Yet you are looking for a way to kill me, because there is no place for my word in you. ³⁸ I am telling you what I have seen at the side of the Father. As for you, you do what you have heard at the side of your father."

³⁹ "Our father is Abraham!" they answered.

"If you were Abraham's children," Jesus told them, "You would do the works of Abraham. ⁴⁰ But now you are looking for a way to kill me, a man who has told you the truth, which I heard at the side of God. Abraham did not do this."

Many of the Jewish people thought their physical descent from Abraham set them free from sin and evil. But only belief in Jesus' words could set them free. Since they did not believe in Jesus, they were bound by the power of sin and unrighteousness. Abraham, unlike many in Jesus' day, looked forward to Jesus' coming. Since Jesus is the Son of God, the Jews who rejected Jesus were also rejecting his Father. All of this was the opposite of what Abraham did.

Luke 3:8

Jesus rebuked the unbelieving Jews:

> ⁸ Therefore produce fruits in keeping with repentance! Do not even think of saying to yourselves, "We have Abraham as our father," because I tell you that God is able to raise up children for Abraham from these stones.

Neither circumcision nor physical descent from Abraham meant anything. Repentance and faith meant everything. All of us, whom God has brought to faith in his Son, can be thankful that we are the stones God has made into true children of Abraham.

Romans 9:6-9

> ⁶ This does not mean that God's word has failed, because not all who are descended from Israel are really Israel, ⁷ and not all who are descended from Abraham are really his children. On the contrary, "Your line of descent will be traced through Isaac." ⁸ This means that it is not the children of the flesh who are God's children, but it is the children of the promise who are counted as his descendants. ⁹ For this is what the promise said: "I will arrive at this set time, and Sarah will have a son."

Many of Abraham's physical descendants had rejected God's promise and were determined to save themselves. This is the human, fleshly way of thinking. Only God's grace can make a person a true child of Abraham, just as only God's grace could enable his promise that Sarah would have a son to come true.

Galatians 3:26-29

> [26] You are all sons of God through faith in Christ Jesus. [27] Indeed, as many of you as were baptized into Christ have been clothed with Christ. [28] There is not Jew or Greek, slave or free, male or female, for you are all one and the same in Christ Jesus. [29] And if you belong to Christ, then you are Abraham's descendants and heirs according to the promise.

This passage gives a perfect summary of what it means to be a child of Abraham. All who are baptized into Christ for the forgiveness of sins are Abraham's descendants and heirs. Such people are the fulfillment of the promise God gave Abraham in Genesis 12:2-3, that all peoples would be blessed in him.

What we learn about Abraham from the New Testament: Paul used Abraham to teach important truths to New Testament believers: Jews and non-Jews become members of God's family through faith alone. We learn that the Mosaic Law did not replace the Gospel promise. We learn the meaning of circumcision, that obedience to God's will always accompanied Old Testament physical circumcision, and that faith in Christ is what makes a person a child of Abraham.

We can only be amazed at the number of important Scriptural truths—truths that we sometimes think are uniquely for the New Testament period—are taught us by this Old Testament figure.

The Conversation

On the very day God commanded Abraham and his household to be circumcised, Abraham carried out the command. There would have been little time to explain. We can only imagine how Abraham's servants were dealing with the event. The characters and the conversation are fictional.

The characters:

Caleb: A servant of Abraham and a mature believer in the true God.

Chloe: Caleb's wife, also a mature believer in the true God.

Abihu: A man who is somewhat skeptical about Abraham's faith.

Anna: Abihu's wife, who shares Abihu's doubts.

Merit: One of the servants Pharaoh gave to Abraham.

> *Abihu*: Well, that was awkward.
>
> *Anna*: I don't even want to think about it.
>
> *Caleb*: It all happened so quickly. When we got up this morning, I had no idea that in a few hours I would be sitting here like this—it hurts.
>
> *Chloe*: I can assure you, the rest of us didn't imagine it either!
>
> *Abihu*: Would someone please tell me what that was all about?
>
> *Caleb*: Well, Abihu, I think Abraham has been telling us about it all along. No, I don't mean why we were circumcised. But how we are to be different from the people around us—why we don't worship with them and why we can't let our children marry theirs.
>
> *Chloe*: When they whisked Caleb away, they said something about God setting us apart from the people around us. If we had not had those worship services, I

CHAPTER 5   Genesis 16,17

would be completely in the dark. I'm still not completely clear, but I think Abraham's faith in the coming Savior is at the heart of it.

Caleb: That's what they told me, too. We were all to receive this mark. It would remind us of who Abraham is—and what we are too.

Abihu: That's simple. We're servants of Abraham. We feed his goats and water his flocks.

Caleb: Are you sure that's all we are, Abihu? The other day, you saw an ax and almost took it. I saw you looking at it. But then you put it down. You picked it up again. But then you put it down again.

Abihu: You're right. I wanted it. But something made me stop.

Chloe: I know what that something is. It's made me stop many times. Every time Abraham tells us about the true God, I cannot help but feel at peace. And every time he explains what the Savior will do, for me, I am so grateful. And when he tells me that his God—our God—considers me to be a righteous person simply because I believe his promise of a Savior, I can't help but do the right thing.

Abihu: Yes, I understand, Chloe. I don't see things as clearly as you and Caleb. Yet I confess, I feel that same peace after our worship services.

Caleb: We are different from the people around us. Their gods give them nothing but demand everything. Our God gives us everything and wants only our hearts. Just think of the blessings he gives our households on account of Abraham. And if God wants to set him apart with this—oh, it still hurts—this circumcision, I'll put up with it.

Merit: I think I'm seeing things more clearly too. It makes me think of my relatives back in Egypt. I know that right now they are giving gifts to this god or that god—the very gods I used to worship. Maybe I'll see them again someday. I might even bring up the topic of circumcision—as gently as I can, of course. It might help me explain my faith in God's promise and the hope I have.

Anna: Well, I have to take care of this guy for the next week! I'll try not to grumble too much.

Closing

This psalm was written after Abraham's descendants were living in the Promised Land of Canaan. In the last verse of this psalm, we are told that the Promised Land was given to the Israelites as a place where they could serve him. God has done the same for us. He has called us into his kingdom, where we, too, can serve the Lord by following his will.

Psalm 105:37-45

> Then he brought Israel out with silver and gold.
> From among their tribes no one stumbled.
> Egypt was glad when they went out,
> > because fear of Israel had fallen on them.
> He spread out a cloud as a canopy
> > and fire to give light at night.
> They asked, and he brought quail,
> > he satisfied them with bread from heaven.
> He opened the rock, and water gushed out.
> It flowed in the desert like a river.

Because he remembered his holy word to Abraham, his
    servant,
He brought out his people with rejoicing,
    his chosen ones with a joyful shout.
He gave them the lands of the nations,
    and they took possession of the work of other
    peoples
    so that they could keep his statutes and observe his
    laws.

Chapter 6
Genesis 18

God Renews His Promise to Abraham—18:1-15
Abraham Prays for Lot—18:16-33

Prayer: Dear Heavenly Father, you have given me many great promises. I confess that at times I am tempted to think it's impossible for some of them to be fulfilled. Use this account to help me put away any doubt that might arise in my heart. Help me take Abraham's and Sarah's actions to heart—to laugh at your promises, not because they are too remarkable to come true, but out of joy that they will. Amen.

Keyword: "Justice" ("Judgment"), [22]
Part One, Justice Leads to Punishment

When sinners hear that God is just and will judge all sins, they become afraid. No one can stand before God and face his justice with the calm feeling that his justice won't reach them.

Genesis 18 and 19 are about how God in justice deals with the wicked, that is, with people who refuse to obey his will.

---

[22] מִשְׁפָּט, the Hebrew word for justice, is pronounced "mish-POT." The "I" is short. The second syllable is pronounced like "pot."

These two chapters are also about God's justice toward those who believe in God's covenant of a Savior and find their righteousness in him.

In chapters six and seven of this book, we will look at the keyword justice (or judgment). In this chapter, we will explore the meaning of God's justice toward the wicked.

God is perfectly just and will judge sinners. There is no escaping that fact. But God is also patient with all people. Earlier in Genesis 15:16, the Lord had promised Abraham to give his descendants the land of Canaan. But it would be several hundred years before they would receive it. He told Abraham why: "Because the guilt of the Amorites is not yet full" (Genesis 15:16). The "Amorites" refers to the inhabitants of the land of Canaan living around Abraham. They were living in sin, and someday God would bring down on them his just judgment in the form of the Israelite occupation of their land. At that time, they and their gods would be destroyed. But in Abraham's day, they still had time to repent.

In Genesis 18, however, the Lord turned his attention to the five cities on the plain around the Jordan River, where Lot had chosen to go when he separated from Abraham. In their case, their time to repent had run out.

As God, the two angels, and Abraham walked along, God told Abraham what he was about to do: "Because the outcry against Sodom and Gomorrah is great, and because their sin is very flagrant, I will go down now and see if what they have done is as bad as the outcry that has come to me. If not, I will know" (Genesis 18:20,21). Were their sins bad enough that God should judge them and punish them? He would get firsthand information and act accordingly.

CHAPTER 6 Genesis 18

God always judges sin. No talk about God's love can overturn that fact. His will is summarized in the Ten Commandments and written on the hearts of every human being. Those who reject God's commands will experience his justice in the form of punishment.

Scripture is filled with warnings about God's judgment on those who rebel against him. Just a few passages that contain the word judge or judgment will make this clear, even though many other passages in Scripture make the same point.

After pointing to the Israelites' many sins, God rebuked them for denying that they were sinners:

> You say, "I am innocent.
> He will not be angry with me."
> But I have indeed judged you
> because you say, "I have not sinned." (Jeremiah 2:35)

In the days of the prophet Ezekiel, God's judgment on the people of Israel was about to begin. Ezekiel prophesied these sobering words:

> An end! The end has come upon the four corners of the land. Now that the end is upon you, I will unleash my anger against you. I will judge you according to your ways, and I will place on you the penalty for all your abominations. My eye will not have pity on you, and I will have no compassion, for I will place on you the penalty for your ways, and the punishment for your abominations will be in your midst. (Ezekiel 7:2-4)

> I, the Lord, have spoken. This is coming, and I will do it. I will not neglect it. I will not spare you, and I will not relent. According to your behavior and your misdeeds, you will be judged, declares the Lord God. (Ezekiel 24:14)

Paul speaks about the wrath God will pour out on those Jews who judged others but refused to acknowledge their own sinfulness. He wrote, "As a result of your stubbornness and your unrepentant heart, you are storing up wrath for yourself on the day of wrath, when God will reveal his righteous judgment" (Romans 2:5). And he foretold what will happen to all those who believe they are saved by keeping the Law: "Now we know that whatever the law says is addressed to those who are under the law, so that every mouth will be silenced and the whole world will be subject to God's judgment" (Romans 5:16).

In 2 Corinthians 5:10, Paul spoke about the final day of judgment: "We must all appear before the judgment seat of Christ, so that each one may receive what is due for what he did while in the body, whether good or bad." This is the essence of God's judgment. Good will be rewarded and evil will be punished.

The Life of Abraham

God Renews His Promise to Abraham—18:1-15

God would soon give Abraham and Sarah a son. We've been building up to that moment. In Genesis 16, we watched Abraham and Sarah try to help God fulfill this promise of a son through the union of Abraham and Sarah's maid, Hagar. Their plan succeeded. Hagar gave birth to Ishmael.

But the fulfillment of God's promises would not depend on their plans. In Genesis 17, God made it clear that Ishmael was not the son of the promise. According to God's plan and by his power, Sarah herself would bear the promised child.

To underline that fact, God changed Abraham and Sarah's names. That name change emphasized that they would be the parents of kings and queens, and that a large nation would be born from them. God then gave Abraham the covenant of circumcision, which set his descendants apart from the other nations of the world.

The events of Genesis 18 took place immediately after this. The LORD—Moses used that special name for God who is faithful to his promises—and two angels in the form of human beings showed up at Abraham's tent.

It was the heat of the day. To Abraham, the three men were normal travelers, and he offered them the normal hospitality he had no doubt shown to others before. Abraham offered the men "a little water" to wash their tired, dusty feet. And he offered to give them "some bread" for their noon meal.

That was certainly a modest description of the meal Abraham and Sarah prepared. While the three men rested during the hot afternoon hours, the household sprang into action. They prepared bread, tender meat, cheese, and milk, and they set them before the men. Abraham stood close by in case the men needed anything.

Then things got interesting. One of the men had a message for Sarah. He would return that same time next year, and Sarah would have a son.

When Sarah heard this, she laughed. By this time, Abraham and Sarah were far too old to have a child. Almost twenty-five years had passed between the time God first promised a son to Abraham and Sarah. Abraham was seventy-five years old when he left Haran, and Sarah was sixty-five. Now Abraham was ninety-nine and Sarah was eighty-nine.

Sarah laughed. One of the men, whom Moses tells us was the LORD, responded: "The LORD said to Abraham, 'Why did Sarah laugh and say, "Will I really give birth to a child though I am old?" Is anything impossible for the LORD? At the set time next year I will return to you, and Sarah will have a son'" (Genesis 18:13,14).

Sarah doubted God and God rebuked her: "Then Sarah denied it and said, 'I did not laugh,' because she was afraid" (Genesis 18:15). God simply said in response, "Yes, you did laugh" (Genesis 18:15). There was no long speech, no lengthy explanation of why she was wrong to doubt—only a short statement that she had in fact laughed. It was a rebuke given to a faithful Christian woman who had momentarily lapsed.

Abraham in the New Testament

Hebrews 13:1-3

> [1] Continue to show brotherly love. [2] Do not fail to show love to strangers, for by doing this some have welcomed angels without realizing it. [3] Remember those in prison, as if you were fellow prisoners, and those who are mistreated, as if you yourselves were also suffering bodily.

There were no interstate signs listing the food places at the next exit or motels where they could spend the night. Travelers were happy to find a home where generous people were watching out for anyone who might pass in need of food and shelter. That was a perfect description of Abraham's home and his generous heart. That example is there for us to imitate.

Luke 1:52-55

> [52] He has brought down rulers from their thrones.

> He has lifted up the lowly.
> ⁵³ He has filled the hungry with good things,
>   but the rich he has sent away empty.
> ⁵⁴ He has come to the aid of his servant Israel,
>   remembering his mercy,
> ⁵⁵as he spoke to our fathers, to Abraham and his
>   offspring forever.

The Old Testament believers knew that Jesus would fulfill God's promises to Abraham. These words are from Mary's song about her son, Jesus. She knew about Abraham and the promises God made to him. She knew those promises had to do with her son, through whom God would show mercy to Abraham's descendants.

Luke 1:68-79

Zechariah, the father of John the Baptist, also described Jesus as the fulfillment of God's oath to Abraham:

> ⁶⁸ Blessed is the Lord, the God of Israel,
>   because he has visited us
>   and prepared redemption for his people.
> ⁶⁹ He has raised up a horn of salvation for us
>   in the house of his servant David,
> ⁷⁰ just as he said long ago
>   through the mouth of his holy prophets.
> ⁷¹ He raised up salvation from our enemies
>   and from the hand of all who hate us,
> ⁷² in order to show mercy to our fathers
>   by remembering his holy covenant,
> ⁷³ the oath which he swore to Abraham our father,
> ⁷⁴ to grant deliverance to us from the hand of our
>   enemies,
>   so that we are able to serve him without fear,
> ⁷⁵in holiness and righteousness before him
>   all our days.

Zechariah's son, John (the Baptist), would teach the people that Jesus would

> 77 ... give his people the knowledge of salvation
> by the forgiveness of their sins,
> 78 because of God's tender mercies,
> by which the Rising Sun from on high will visit us,
> 79 to shine on those who sit in darkness
> and in the shadow of death,
> to guide our feet into the way of peace.

Zechariah was speaking about the redemption that God had promised to Abraham, which all God's people were waiting for. Zechariah linked Abraham to Jesus through King David, a descendant of Abraham and an ancestor of Jesus. He also mentioned the Old Testament prophets, who foretold the Savior's birth.

Like Mary, Zechariah understood the difference between the wicked and the righteous. Jesus was the horn—the power—to save the righteous from the wicked. Because believers are holy and righteous in God's eyes through Christ, we can serve the Lord in holiness and righteousness. We can also serve the Lord without being afraid of those who try to stop us.

Both Mary and Zechariah were Old Testament believers who lived on the cusp of the New Testament. Their songs are important because they show us what all Old Testament believers—true children of Abraham—were looking forward to. They looked ahead to the time when "the Rising Sun" would shine on them by giving them "the forgiveness of sins" and guiding their feet "into the way of peace."

What we learn about Abraham from the New Testament: All Old Testament believers shared the hope given in God's promises to Abraham. As evidenced by Mary's and Zechariah's songs, they understood the foundation of God's salvation, namely, the forgiveness of sins.

The Conversation

This conversation is between Hagar and Sarah sometime after the destruction of Sodom and Gomorrah. It gives us a glimpse of how Ishmael would soon mistreat Isaac. This conversation is fictional, but the characters are real.

The characters:

Sarah: Abraham's wife

Hagar: Sarah's servant and the mother of Ishmael

Ishmael: Hagar's son, who is about thirteen years old at this time

> *Sarah:* Hagar, I'm so thankful to have you with me.
>
> *Hagar:* Sarah, I confess I was out of line when I first got pregnant. I looked down on you because you couldn't have a child and I could.
>
> *Sarah:* That's OK. You've been nothing but a joy and a help since you came back.
>
> *Hagar:* Now we will both have sons. I have Ishmael. I know your son will be the heir of the promises God gave to Abraham. But Ishmael will be a powerful man, and great nations will come from him also. I look forward to watching him grow and become as powerful as God said he would be.
>
> *Sarah:* I'm glad for you. You were part of our plan to fulfill God's promise, and I resented you when you

became pregnant. But we should have known that God didn't need our help. How old I am! And Abraham—what can I say? But God just told us that I will become pregnant, and quite soon.

Ishmael: I don't want a brother! It's me and Dad. He loves me and I love him.

Hagar: But Ishmael, he'll be your brother. Your father will love both of you the same.

Ishmael: But look what I can do. I'm stronger than any of the kids around here. I can shoot an arrow better than most of those so-called soldiers Father keeps around. And I'm starting stone slinging lessons. And then fighting sticks. And then swords. Nobody will stop me.

Hagar: Don't talk like that. It sounds like you're looking for a fight. Your father wouldn't talk like that.

Ishmael: I want to be the greatest. Father says I will be. He never lies.

Hagar: Ishmael, your father loves you. He thought you were going to pass on the blessings God gave to him. And he wanted you to. But last year—remember when you were circumcised—God told your father that Sarah's son would receive God's special blessings. But he also said great things about you. He will bless you. Some of your children will be powerful leaders. And God will make you into a great nation, just like he'll do for Sarah's son. So you have nothing to be afraid of. You and your brother can be friends.

Ishmael: "I'm not afraid of anybody. Nobody can be better than me. Nobody will get in my way, especially some little kid."

Sarah: Ishmael, your mother and I both love you. I'm sure everything will turn out all right.

The Life of Abaham

Abraham Prays for Lot—18:16-33

The scene shifts abruptly. We are no longer watching afternoon travelers enjoying their rest. Thoughts of God's merciful promise to bless Abraham with a child are momentarily set aside.

As Abraham walked with his guests to see them on their way, the LORD asked the two angels if he should tell Abraham what he was about to do. The answer was yes. Abraham needed to be a part of the events of the next few days. And it was not just for curiosity's sake. Or even because it would affect his nephew Lot. It was because of the important role God had given Abraham.

God explained, "All the nations of the earth will be blessed in him. For I have chosen him, so that he may command his children and his household who follow after him to keep the way of the LORD by carrying out righteousness and justice, so that the LORD may deliver to Abraham what he has promised him" (Genesis 18:17-19).

Abraham would become a great person. All people would be blessed in him and in his seed. In chapter 5, we heard Paul explain that Abraham's seed did not refer to the large number of descendants who would be born from him. Rather, it referred to Christ. Before Christ was born, however, Abraham's many descendants would also have an important role to play. They were to be witnesses to the world of the true God and his promise.

To do that successfully, they needed someone to train them. The events about to unfold regarding Sodom and Gomorrah—how God responded to Abraham's prayer and God's judgment on the wicked—would teach Abraham important lessons he could pass on to his descendants.

To help us understand what God was teaching Abraham, consider the work of John the Baptist. God commissioned him to prepare the way for the Lord. He did this in two ways. He told everyone that they were sinners and needed a Savior. Then he pointed to Jesus and said that he was the Lamb of God who would take away the sins of the world. He urged the people to repent and be baptized for the forgiveness of sins. Using this message of sin and grace, John could fulfill his role of preparing people for the arrival of the promised Savior.

The events of the next couple of days would teach Abraham these same truths. He was led to pray that God would spare the cities. In the process, he would learn much about God's mercy and patience. He would also learn that God does, in fact, answer prayer to save the righteous. And he would experience firsthand God's punishment on unrighteousness and unrepentance. This experience would help Abraham teach these truths to his descendants so they would daily repent of their sins and serve the Lord in righteousness.

These accounts teach us the same thing. They teach us about God's final judgment on those who reject his promises, who live apart from him, and who serve sin. They teach us to pray for the righteous, confident that God will deliver them.

When Abraham heard what God was about to do, his heart went out to Lot and his family. He also wondered if other righteous people might be living there, and he prayed for them. It was not unreasonable for Abraham to think this. Remember that years earlier, five kings from the East had attacked those cities and carried off their people and goods. Abraham and his little army went after them to rescue Lot. In the process, they rescued all the other captives and their belongings. When Abraham met Melchizedek in the city of Salem, the king of Sodom was there. He and all the inhabitants of the five cities had a chance to meet Abraham, witness the honor he showed to Melchizedek, and listen to Melchizedek thank God for delivering Abraham. They witnessed Abraham honor God by refusing to keep the spoils of war. They learned what it meant to be a follower of God and that God gives peace to the righteous by providing for them and protecting them.

Perhaps some had taken this experience with Abraham and Melchizedek to heart and repented of their wickedness. This was a possibility, so Abraham asked God to spare the cities for their sake. Were there fifty who might have come to faith in the true God? No, there were not fifty. How about forty? No. Lower and lower Abraham set the bar until he reached ten. Despite everything Abraham had done for them and despite everything they had seen and heard, they refused to repent and seek God. Rather, they sunk deeper and deeper into sinful depravity.

When Abraham heard that there were fewer than ten believers in the city of Sodom, it became clear that Lot and his family were the only believers there. At that, Abraham left things in God's hands and returned home.

Closing

God's promises are sure. Despite the difficulties God's church endures, these difficulties are never a sign that God has forsaken it.

Jeremiah 33:23-26

> Have you not considered what these people are saying
> > that the Lord rejected the two families that he chose?
>
> They despise my people in this way,
> > and they do not consider them a nation.
>
> The Lord says: If I have not established my covenant
> > with day and night,
> > or the ordinances of heaven and earth,
>
> only then will I reject the offspring of Jacob
> > and of my servant David,
>
> only then will I fail to choose one of his sons
> > to rule over the offspring of Abraham, Isaac, and Jacob.
>
> So I will restore them from captivity,
> > and I will have mercy on them.

Chapter 7
Genesis 19

God Answers Abraham's Prayer to Spare Lot—19:1-29
It Is Dangerous to Live Close to Unbelief—19:30-38

Prayer: Dear Lord, sin infects your world and everyone who lives in it. Because I have a sinful nature, sin is also a part of my life. Help me learn to avoid living as the world lives, with all its allurements and unbelieving pitfalls. Help me learn to be like Abraham, who prayed on behalf of fellow believers and helped them escape from the destruction that awaits all who turn away from you. Amen.

Keyword: "Justice" ("Judgment")
Part Two, Justice Ends with Mercy

No sin remains hidden from God. And God sweeps no sin under the rug. As we saw in the keyword section in the last chapter, no sin goes unpunished. God justly condemns everyone who sins, and he sentences them to an eternity apart from him in the suffering of Hell.

But God made a covenant with mankind. He promised to undergo the punishment we deserve rather than make us bear the suffering ourselves. Simply put, he sent someone else to suffer for our sins in our place. That was the Savior God promised to Adam and Eve, who would crush Satan's power by taking away his right to accuse us before God.

God repeated this promise to Abraham and Sarah. The Savior would come from Abraham, and for that reason, Abraham would be a blessing to the whole world. Through faith in God's promise, God considered Abraham to be a righteous person. And Abraham responded by serving and obeying God. Because of the promise, there are now two groups of people, the righteous and the wicked.

As we heard in Genesis 18, Abraham made a sharp distinction between the righteous and the wicked when he prayed for Sodom and Gomorrah. Abraham was not asking God to weigh the number of *good people* in the cities against the number of *bad people* there. Rather, he was asking God to weigh the number of people who were righteous by faith against the number of people who had rejected God.

Indeed, the morals of the wicked were very different from the morals of the righteous. The righteous served God because they knew and loved him, and because the wicked didn't know God or care about him, they lived for greed and lust. Because Abraham understood this—that the righteous are saved through faith in God's promise—he could ask God to show them his mercy and hold off judging them. Abraham knew that God punishes sin. But he also knew that God withholds his punishment from those, who, like him, were righteous through faith in the Savior.

Consider the following passages in which the writers rejoice in God's justice and judgments. If the writers were speaking about God's judgment on the wicked, the passages would make no sense. But if the writers were referring to God's just mercy on believers, then they make perfect sense, and we can rejoice in what they say.

> Your praise, O God, reaches to the ends of the earth,
> just as your fame does.
> Righteousness fills your right hand.
> Mount Zion rejoices.
> The daughters of Judah *celebrate because of your judgments.* (Psalm 48:9-11)

The next passage lists God's many blessings—pardon, healing, eternal redemption, mercy, and compassion. God is just to give these blessings to people who are in Christ.

> Bless the Lord, O my soul,
> and do not forget all his benefits—
> who pardons all your guilt,
> who heals all your diseases,
> who redeems your life from the pit,
> who crowns you with mercy and compassion,
> who satisfies your life with goodness,
> so that your youth is renewed like the eagle.
> The Lord performs righteousness *and justice* for all the oppressed. (Psalm 103:2-6)

Israel had refused to follow the Lord, but the Lord eagerly wanted to show them his justice and mercy:

> This is what the Lord God, the Holy One of Israel, says:
> If you repent and wait quietly, you will be saved.
> Your strength will depend on quietness and trust.
> But you refused....
> But the Lord is eager to be gracious to you.
> *He waits on high to have mercy on you,*
> *for the Lord is a God of justice.*
> Blessed are all those who long for him.
> (Isaiah 30:15-18)

The Savior's work resulted in justice, something that will make all people rejoice. In the next verse, God's *law* refers to his will to show mercy, not to his Ten Commandments.

> Here is my servant, whom I uphold,
> > my chosen one in whom I delight.
> I am placing my Spirit on him.
> He will announce *a just verdict for the nations.*
> He will not cry out.
> He will not raise his voice.
> He will not make his voice heard in the street.
> A bent reed he will not break,
> > and a dimly burning wick he will not snuff out.
> *He will faithfully bring forth a just verdict.*
> He will not burn out, and he will not be broken
> > until he establishes justice on the earth.
> The coastlands will wait for *his law.* (Isaiah 42:1-4)

In the next verse, God tells us to boast that we know three things about him—that he is merciful, that he justly forgives our sins, and that everything he does is right.

> This is what the LORD says.
> The wise man should not boast in his wisdom.
> The strong man should not boast in his strength,
> > nor the rich man in his riches.
> Instead, let those who boast boast about this:
> > that they have understanding, and that they know me.
> They know that I am the LORD,
> > *who shows mercy, justice, and righteousness on earth,*
> for I delight in these things, declares the LORD.
> (Jeremiah 9:23,24)

If we imagine that God's justice always results in punishment, we will not understand the next verse. Here Jeremiah contrasts God's justice with his anger. He asks God to correct him, but to correct him in mercy for Christ's sake, and not in anger over his sin. That is the just thing to do.

> I know, LORD, that a man's way is not his own,
>   nor can a man direct his own steps.
> *Correct me, LORD, but with justice,*
>   *not in your anger,*
>   or you will reduce me to nothing.
> (Jeremiah 10:23,24)

Abraham understood God's justice—punishment for the wicked but blessing for the righteous. God's justice was the basis of his prayer for the righteous people who might be living in Sodom and Gomorrah. He started his prayer like this:

> What if there are fifty righteous people in the city? Will you really sweep them away and not spare the place for the sake of the fifty righteous who are in it? You would never do such a thing, killing the righteous along with the wicked, treating the righteous the same as the wicked. You would never do such a thing. *The Judge* of all the earth should do right, shouldn't he? (Genesis 18:24,25)

But because everyone in the five cities had forsaken God, refused to repent, and sunk so deeply into sin, it was time for God in justice to condemn them. Abraham understood that. God would use another way to answer his prayer and, in justice, spare any righteous people still in the cities.

The Life of Abraham

God Answers Abraham's Prayer to Spare Lot—19:1-29

The two angels entered Sodom. Lot was waiting at the city gate for anyone who might want to stay the night in the city.

The two angels showed up, and Lot treated them just like Abraham had—with the utmost respect. The men refused his offer of lodging, but Lot pressed them. They agreed and followed him home. Again, just like Abraham, he prepared a feast. We see Lot's faith in action.

God said that the outcry against Sodom and Gomorrah was great. He had sent the angels to find out just how bad it was. It didn't take long. We soon realize why Lot had been so insistent that the men stay at his house. Before the group turned in for the night, the men of the town, both young and old, assembled at his door and demanded that Lot send the two men out so they could have sex with them.

There was no doubt the city would not repent. We sometimes forget how richly God had blessed them. Abraham had saved them from the five kings of the East. Note again what they had seen and heard. They had witnessed the miracle of Abraham's victory. They had seen and heard the exchange between Abraham and Melchizedek. They had seen Abraham refuse to take the plunder. All this seems to have rolled off their backs. Within a few years, they had gone back to their former immorality. Perhaps they had even become worse.

Lot refused the men's demand to send out the two visitors. Instead, he offered his two daughters and permitted the men to do with them what they wanted. It is hard to imagine how a father could do this. Even the sacred nature of caring for guests in one's home doesn't excuse him. However, the real question is why Lot put himself in a situation where he had to make that choice.

CHAPTER 7   Genesis 19

It Is Dangerous to Live Close to Unbelief—19:30-38

God now knew how wicked the city was, and the angels had their command to destroy it.

It was time for Lot's family to leave. The two angels pulled Lot back inside the house and struck the men of Sodom with blindness. They hurriedly tried to locate other members of Lot's family. Lot tried to persuade his future sons-in-law to go with him, but they thought he was joking.

In the morning, the men urged Lot to leave before the destruction began. From that point on, we see a family torn between worldly desires and God's attempt to save them. The angels had to pull them out physically. They told the family to flee to the mountains lest they be swept up in the Lord's punishment on the cities. Lot hesitated, as did his wife and daughters. They would have to leave the comforts of home. But the angels told them to run and not look back.

The angels gave Lot a simple command. But Lot had other ideas. If the Lord would perhaps spare the smallest of the cities, Zoar, he and his family could live there. The angels gave him permission to do that.

But Lot's logic did not include God. If God had spared Lot from the destruction he brought on Sodom, there was no reason why God would let him die in the mountains. What's more, it made no sense to think that Zoar was any more God-fearing than Sodom, and the other four cities. Sometime during the flight, Lot's wife succumbed to thoughts about the physical things she was leaving behind. She looked back at what she was losing, and God turned her into a pillar of salt.

Lot reached Zoar early in the morning. When he was safe, the angels destroyed Sodom and the other cities. Lot and his daughters tried to live in Zoar, but for some reason, the people of the town didn't want them there. So he did what he had been told to do in the first place. He fled to the mountains.

What happens next shows just how much Lot gave up by moving to Sodom. All those years, his daughters had been watching his propensity to rely on himself. They had been living among immoral people whose homosexual lusts were never far below the surface. They had watched their father choose to live in this environment rather than give up the advantages of city life. They had just heard their father bypass trust in God to protect the strangers who were lodging with him, offering them, his own daughters, to a mob of men to use as sex toys.

We are not told, but they must have known their father's uncle Abraham, who for so long had relied on God to give him a child. If only they had followed his example! But life in Sodom hardly fostered trust in the Lord's care. The three of them were alone, living in a cave in the mountains. The women had been betrothed, but the men had refused to leave Sodom. Humanly speaking, there was little hope for them to have a husband and children.

So they used their father Lot. Each got him drunk and had sex with him. Lot's act of straying from the good spiritual environment Abraham could have provided for him and choosing to live among the godless had borne its fruit. And sadly, the memory of these acts would stay alive in the names of their two sons, Moab and Ammon. They were both fathers of nations who were close neighbors of the Israelites, and their names can be found throughout the Old Testament.

Lot in the New Testament

2 Peter 2:6-9

> ⁶ If God condemned the cities of Sodom and Gomorrah to destruction, by turning them into ashes when he made them an example of things to come for the ungodly; ⁷ and if he rescued righteous Lot, who was very distressed by the unrestrained immorality of the wicked people ⁸ (while that righteous man was living among them, he was tormented in his righteous soul day after day by the lawless deeds he saw and heard); ⁹ then the Lord knows how to deliver the godly out of temptation and to keep the unrighteous under guard until the day of judgment, in order to punish them.

In this and the previous chapter, our keyword was "judgment." Peter says that the destruction of Sodom and Gomorrah is "an example of things to come for the ungodly." The account of Sodom and Gomorrah reminds us that God will someday judge this ungodly world and completely destroy it.

The account of Lot, however, teaches us about God's merciful judgment on believers. Through faith in Christ's forgiveness, we are righteous. God has promised us an eternal home with him in Heaven. Therefore, when he judges the world by destroying it, he will also judge believers by rescuing them.

Lot had not lost his faith. He still worshipped God and was a righteous person, as Peter says. He knew God's promise to Abraham, and he believed it. We saw evidence of his faith when he insisted that the two travelers lodge at his house rather than stay in the public square and face the homosexual lust of the men of the town.

But living in Sodom brought temptation and spiritual anxiety into the lives of Lot and his family. This is a warning for us. It is dangerous to live close to the sins of unbelievers. There is always the temptation to forsake God.

However, Peter's purpose in the verses above is to demonstrate God's great mercy and patience. He wrote, "If he rescued righteous Lot, who was very distressed by the unrestrained immorality of the wicked people, . . . then the Lord knows how to deliver the godly out of temptation" (2 Peter 2:7,9). By living in Sodom, Lot put himself in a bad situation. Their wickedness distressed him. He continually witnessed unrestrained immorality. He knew his neighbors were committing terrible sins against God's law. Their actions contradicted everything he knew was right and every way he wanted to serve God.

We are tempted to criticize Lot, and we have every reason to. He should have gotten himself and his family out of there. But God had patience. He kept Lot from succumbing to the wickedness around him. And when it was time to destroy Sodom, he delivered Lot.

We must confess that we have sometimes done the same as Lot. The scenes we watch on TV, in a movie, or in a video game, what we listen to in audiobooks or experience at certain parties and venues where we shouldn't be—this makes us residents of Sodom. We are thankful that the Lord, who knew how to protect and deliver Lot, knows how to deliver us.

Even when we try to flee from Sodom, we find ourselves trapped there, not by choice but because on this side of Heaven there is no perfect escape. Paul says in 1 Corinthians 5:9-10: "When I wrote to you in my letter not to associate with the sexually immoral, I did not at all mean the sexually immoral people of this world, or the greedy and swindlers, or idolaters, for then you would have to leave the world." Regardless of what Lot could have done to mitigate exposure to the sins of unbelievers, and regardless of what we can do, all believers must still live among those who disobey God.

If God can deliver Lot with all his weaknesses, he can deliver us, too. Abraham had prayed that God save the righteous by not destroying the cities. But there weren't even ten righteous people to save. So God pulled Lot out of Sodom before he destroyed it. God will not deliver this world by foregoing its destruction. Instead, he will deliver the righteous by taking us out of this world before it is destroyed.

Luke 17:26-33

> [26] Just as it was in the days of Noah, so will it also be in the days of the Son of Man. [27] They were eating and drinking, marrying and being given in marriage, until the day when Noah entered the ark. Then the flood came and destroyed them all. [28] Likewise, just as it was in the days of Lot: They were eating and drinking, buying and selling, planting and building, [29] but on the day when Lot went out from Sodom, fire and sulfur rained down from heaven and destroyed them all. [30] It will be the same on the day the Son of Man is revealed. [31] On that day, the person who is on the roof and has belongings in the house should not go down to get them. Likewise, the person in the field should not turn back for anything. [32] Remember Lot's wife! [33] Whoever

tries to preserve his life will lose it, but whoever loses his life will keep it.

God physically delivered Lot's wife from Sodom, but mentally, a part of her was still there. Jesus warns us to live with a view to Judgment Day. We are to give up our lives in this world and set our minds completely on "the city that has foundations, whose architect and builder is God," like Abraham did (Hebrews 11:10).

What we learn about Lot from the New Testament: Lot was a righteous man. He had many weaknesses, and he was too often driven by his sinful nature. Yet he shared Abraham's faith, and God graciously delivered him from the judgment on the wicked.

The Conversation

This conversation is about a hypothetical event that may have happened after the destruction of Sodom and Gomorrah. It is based on Martin Luther's speculation that Abraham found Lot and invited him to live at this home.[23] If Abraham had risked his life to fight the four kings when they captured Lot, it is not hard to imagine Abraham trying to find out if Lot was still alive. Eliezer and Abraham are real people. Caleb is fictional.

The characters:

Eliezar: The manager of Abraham's household.

Caleb: Abraham's servant and a mature believer in God.

Abraham

---

[23] Martin Luther, *Luther's Works*, Vol. 3, (St. Louis, Concordia Publishing House, 1961), p. 312.

A woman from Zoar: Zoar is where Lot first went after he left Sodom.

Eliezar: Caleb, Abraham has decided to see if Lot is OK. He saw the smoke going up from Sodom and Gomorrah last week. He's been fretting over Lot ever since. He wonders if someone has seen him. He doesn't think that's likely, but he has to find out. Abraham has asked me to go along and help him look. I'm glad he did. A hundred-year-old man shouldn't be left alone.

Caleb: Where will you start?

Eliezar: Someone passed through here the other day. He told us that the four big towns had been completely destroyed but that the little one, Zoar, had been spared. We'll start there.

Abraham: Let's see if anyone has seen him. Eliezar, ask this woman.

Woman from Zoar: Yes, we saw him briefly. He was happy to be here. He was here with two younger women—no one else.

Eliezar: Is he still here?

Woman from Zoar: No. Some thought he was the reason why the cities were destroyed. I guess he was afraid and left. I saw them head toward those mountains.

Abraham: Then we'll go there.

Eliezar: Sir, it will be like looking for a needle in a haystack.

Abraham: I know, but I love Lot. By God's grace, he is a righteous man. And so is his family. But they are weak. Maybe I can help them.

Eliezar, after several days of looking for Lot: Abraham, we've been looking for days and haven't found him. The shepherds around here haven't seen him either. We've tried the shelters he might have used. Nothing. And do you know how many caves there are in these hills? He could be in any one of them.

Abraham: Very well. Let's go home. We will pray that God continues to protect him. And how can we doubt that he will? If God saved Lot from Sodom, he will be with him now. Maybe he'll look to us for help. He knows our love for him.

Closing

As you read these verses, remember that God has chosen you like he chose Abraham and will keep you safe from those who oppose you.

Isaiah 41:8-13

> But you, O Israel, my servant,
> O Jacob, whom I have chosen,
>> the offspring of Abraham, whom I love,
>> whom I have snatched from the ends of the earth,
>> whom I have called from its corners—
> I have said to you, "You are my servant."
> I have chosen you and not rejected you.
> Do not fear, for I am with you.
> Do not be overwhelmed, for I am your God.
> I will strengthen you. Yes, I will help you.
> I will uphold you with my righteous right hand.
> Just watch, they will be ashamed and humiliated—all

>   those who are angry with you.
> They will become nothing and perish—
>   those men who oppose you.
> You will look for them, but you will not find them—
>   those men who contend against you.
> They will become absolutely nothing, less than nothing—
>   those men who battle against you.
> For I am the Lord your God.
> I am the one who is holding on to your right hand.
> I am the one who says to you, "Do not fear. I myself am helping you."

Chapter 8
Genesis 20,21

Abraham Meets Abimelek, Part One—20:1-18
God Fulfills His Promise: Isaac is born—21:1-21
Abraham Meets Abimelek, Part Two—21:22-34

Prayer: Dear Heavenly Father, help me wait patiently for you to fulfill your promises. I know that your promises will come true because it is you who have made them. Unfulfilled promises lead many to doubt. But may all your promises, whether they are fulfilled yet or not, strengthen my faith and give me further resolve to put all my trust in you. Amen.

Keyword: "Holiness" [24]

In Scripture, God is described by another keyword, "holiness." When we think of God's holiness, we often think of his moral perfection. In his Ten Commandments, God tells us what is right and wrong. He threatens to punish everyone who does not keep his commandments and will bless those who do.

That is true. But it is not the only way Scripture defines God's holiness. The basic definition of holiness is "to be set

---

[24] The word for holy is קָדוֹשׁ. It is pronounced Ka-DOSH. The "a" is short and the "o" is long.

apart." That definition will help us better understand what it means that God is holy.

Just as God is set apart from all immorality, God's way of dealing with people is set apart from how human religions and their gods deal with their followers. All man-made religions deal with their followers on the basis of obedience to the law. But from the beginning, God promised to deal with all people on the basis of the forgiveness of sins acquired by his Son's blood. All human religions and their gods demand things from their followers and give them nothing in return. But the true God, who satisfied his own demand that we be perfect, wants nothing more than to give us every good thing. All human gods have evil characteristics and cannot be fully trusted by their followers. The true God is perfect, and his followers can trust him implicitly.

God's holiness is like the other keywords we have looked at. Those words can be considered either apart from God's promise of a Savior or with that promise in mind. God's glory could make us afraid because no mortal can stand face to face with God in all his glory. Yet God's glory also is his infinite love and compassion toward those who believe his covenant promise. God's righteousness always scares a person when that person compares God's perfect righteousness with their own imperfect righteousness. But believers know that they are righteous through faith in God's Savior, and that gives them peace in God's presence. The thought of God's judgment always makes sinners afraid until they come to faith in Christ's victory over their sins. They are then sure that the holy God judges them as innocent people.

In Isaiah 6, the prophet Isaiah heard the angels in Heaven cry out "Holy, holy, holy is the LORD of Armies! The whole earth is full of his glory!" (Isaiah 6:3). Isaiah could only respond, "I am doomed! I am ruined, because I am a man with unclean lips, and I dwell among a people with unclean lips, and because my eyes have seen the King, the LORD of Armies!" (Isaiah 6:5). Isaiah had a problem when he found himself in the presence of the holy God! Until, that is, God sent an angel with a live coal in his hands and touched Isaiah's lips with it and said, "Look, this has touched your lips, so your guilt is taken away, and your sin is forgiven" (Isaiah 6:7). When the holy God asked who would be willing to take his word to the people of Israel, because his lips had been cleansed and set apart, Isaiah could be bold to say, "Here I am. Send me!" (Isaiah 6:8).

In 1 Samuel 2:1,2. Hannah had just given her son Samuel to the LORD for full-time work at the temple. She sang a song of praise to God: "There is *no one holy like the Lord*. Yes, there is no one but you, and there is no rock like our God" (1 Samuel 2:2). Hannah praised God by confessing that there is no one like him. He is completely set apart from all other gods; that is, he is set apart from the legalistic way that people think a god should act—people who have fashioned gods in their own image.

A more difficult passage combines God's holiness with two of his other characteristics:

> But the LORD of Armies is exalted by justice,
> and God, the Holy One, reveals his holiness by righteousness. (Isaiah 5:16)

In this verse, Isaiah combines three words: justice, righteousness, and holiness. He says that God's justice is unlike the justice of human beings and their gods, who are self-centered and unconcerned about treating others fairly. He also speaks about God's perfect righteousness, namely, his ability to do everything right. He is unlike human beings and their gods, who find it impossible to do the right thing or be a source of blessing to the world. God's perfect justice and righteousness reveal his holiness. That is, they show that God is set apart from the way sinful human beings and their gods act and think.

Isaiah invited all people to enjoy the everlasting covenant, "the faithful mercies promised to David." When God fulfilled his covenant, people from all nations would run to the Israelites to learn about "the Holy One of Israel."

> Hey, all of you who are thirsty, come to the water,
>   even if you have no money!
> Come, buy and eat!
> Come, buy wine and milk without money and without
>   cost.
> Why do you spend money on something that is not
>   bread?
> Why do you waste your labor on something that does
>   not satisfy?
> Listen carefully to me, and eat what is good.
> Satisfy your appetite with rich food.
> Turn your ear toward me, and come to me.
> Listen, so that you may continue to live.
> Yes, I will make *an everlasting covenant with you,*
>   *the faithful mercies promised to David.*
> Look, I appointed him as a witness for peoples,
>   a leader and commander of peoples.
> Look, you will call out to a nation you do not know,
>   and a nation that does not know you will run to
>   you,
>   on account of the Lord your God,
>   because of *the Holy One of Israel,*
>   for he has glorified you. (Isaiah 55:1-5)

Using the same word, holy, Peter describes what God has made us to be. He said, "But you are a chosen people, a royal priesthood, *a holy nation*, the people who are God's own possession, so that you may proclaim the praises of him who called you out of darkness into his marvelous light" (1 Peter 2:9). Peter is contrasting our former condition with the fact that God has made us his holy people, set apart from the world and set apart for his service. God's holiness did the same for Abraham.

The Conversation

In this conversation, Eliezar and Caleb talk about the times when Abraham seemed to doubt God's promises. Eliezer was a real person while Caleb is fictional.

The characters:

Eliezar: The manager of Abraham's household.

Caleb: One of Abraham's servants, a mature believer in the true God.

> *Caleb:* It's been quite a rough ride for Abraham and Sarah. Promises that humanly speaking are impossible to fulfill. Life in a land that doesn't belong to them. Hearing God's repeated promise to make him into a great nation, but childless at 100 years old with a ninety-year-old wife. And now, three men have just come to Abraham and told him he's a year away from having a child. I can just imagine what my wife would say if someone told her at ninety that in a year, she'd have a son! Sarah just laughed, but my wife would probably laugh and then show the guy to the door.

Eliezar: I've been with Abraham and Sarah for a long time. I was with them long before they left our home in Haran. I've watched them obey what God told them to do. I've heard Abraham speak so often about God's promises with such confidence that it removes my own doubt. But I've seen him act in some very surprising ways. Sometimes I have to shake my head.

Caleb: What do you mean, Eliezar?

Eliezar: God said he would protect Abraham, right? And that whoever blessed him would be blessed, and whoever cursed him would be cursed. That sounds like he would keep Abraham perfectly safe. And that's what Abraham says to us when we worship the Lord at his altars. But then we had to live in Egypt during that famine....

Caleb: Yes, I know. He told people that Sarah was his sister.

Eliezar: So he wouldn't be killed. But where was his confidence in God's promises then?

Caleb: And the way he made Pharaoh suffer!

Eliezar: But on the other hand, I think about the time he let Lot choose whatever land he wanted. Lot took advantage of the situation, but Abraham didn't care. He had no doubt that God would bless him. He knew he would someday have the whole land for himself.

Caleb: Which reminds me of another time. You know how confident he was in God's promises when he took his little army and chased those four kings and beat them. Believe me, I saw it happen. Abraham didn't flinch when the attack came, and his tactics were brilliant. Then he returned with all that plunder. But he wouldn't take any of it for himself. All because he wanted to let God make him wealthy, not some local king.

Eliezar: Abraham once told me that God promised him a son and many offspring. But at the same time, he told God that I was going to inherit his estate. It's like he didn't remember what God had promised him. But still, when God told him to look at the stars, because that's how many descendants would come from his body, without flinching, Abraham took God at his word.

But right after that, he wanted proof that his descendants would own the land of Canaan as God promised. He said to God—and I heard him say it—"How do I know I'll own this land?" I helped him prepare some animals—you know, like you do when you're going to make a treaty. Abraham told me later that God used those animals to repeat his promise. Then God told him about the difficult times in store for his people and that it would be many years before the promise was fulfilled. But God said he would fulfill the promise all by himself. He didn't need anybody's help.

Caleb: I remember what happened next. The two of them used Hagar to fulfill God's promise. They just couldn't wait. They doubted that God could do it on his own.

Eliezar: And then came Ishmael. Oh, how Abraham loved that boy. To Abraham, Ishmael was the promised son. He was Abraham's heir and the father of the great nation God had promised him. I can't blame him and Sarah for doing that, especially as the years went on.

Hagar was young and fertile. Sarah was old and barren. But still. . . .

Caleb: Sarah shared her husband's faith. But she surprised me when those three travelers came by that one day. One of them said she would have a son. She just laughed. You know, there was doubt in that laugh, and the visitor recognized it.

Eliezar: I just heard that we're moving southwest into Philistine territory. Maybe things will go better there. Maybe Abraham and Sarah have overcome their doubts.

The Life of Abraham

Abraham Meets Abimelek, Part One—20:1-18

Scripture always speaks about Abraham's love for God's promise of a Savior, and about his faith in that promise. So, we might think that Abraham's sin of lying to Pharaoh was a one-time event. But this account tells us that Abraham's fear of losing his life over Sarah lingered on.

This account is similar to Abraham's visit to Egypt. In both cases, Abraham lied to a ruler about Sarah, saying that she was his sister. He did this to protect himself. Sarah was desirable as a wife, and both rulers took her into their homes.

But the accounts are different.

The trip to Egypt was relatively early in Abraham's life in Canaan. He had God's promise of a son. But he still didn't know that Sarah would be the birth mother. The present account comes much later. God had just told Abraham that Sarah would become pregnant and that they would have a son the following year. Still, Abraham told Abimelek that

Sarah was his sister, and Abimelek innocently took her as his wife.

But like he did in Egypt, Abraham put the promise in jeopardy. There's a real chance that if God had not intervened, Abimelek might not have let her go back to Abraham.

From the earlier account of Melchizedek and his followers, we know that in Canaan there were believers in the true God. Abimelek was one. After he took Sarah as his wife, God came to him in a dream and told him the truth about Sarah. Abimelek immediately expressed his shock, and he asserted his innocence.

God told Abimelech that he had kept him away from Sarah. At the end of the account, we are told that God had shut up the wombs of all the women in Abimelek's household. Perhaps this was an illness and had something to do with how God kept Abimelech away from Sarah. However, there was another way this illness helped preserve God's promise. We, the readers, know that Sarah was barren and could not have had a child by Abimelek. But those outside Abraham's family didn't know that. So by making all the women in Abimelek's household barren, God erased from everyone's mind all thoughts that Abimelek might be Isaac's father. After all, Sarah would give birth to Isaac within the year.

Abimelek didn't want anyone to think he had knowingly sinned against God by unlawfully taking Sarah as his wife. So he gave Abraham a large sum of money as a public witness that he had no relations with Sarah.

Abraham had set a terrible example. He should have trusted in God to protect him and not lied. And you think that God would have told Abraham to apologize to Abimelek for deceiving him. But God did not do that. As in the case of Pharaoh, God put the burden on Abimelek. He had to take the initiative and ask Abraham to pray that God spare his life. Note the irony of the situation: The man who sinfully caused Abimelek to sin was to pray that God spare Abimelek from the sin that he, Abraham, had led him to commit.

Abraham was also wrong in predetermining that Abimelek was a godless person from whom he needed to protect himself. We might give Abraham some slack in this case. He had just found out that there were no righteous people in Sodom and Gomorrah. What were the odds, he might have thought, that the people of Gerar were any different? Yet, when Abraham discovered the opposite—that Abimelek was an upright man—he could have been more gracious. When Abimelek asked Abraham what he'd done to deserve such treatment, rather than asking for Abimelek's forgiveness, Abraham blithely excused himself: He feared being killed over Sarah, so in those situations he always called her his sister.

Was there no other way to keep himself safe than by lying and putting in jeopardy Sarah's place as his wife and mother of his son? Was there no other way than to make God afflict with diseases anyone who took Sarah as his wife?

Regardless, God protected Abraham and Sarah, and in the process, he protected his promise that Abraham would be a blessing to all nations, including the people of Gerar. In no uncertain terms, he upheld Abraham's position in his plan for the world and made Abimelek subservient to him. Abimelek and his household would be spared God's anger only if Abraham prayed to God on their behalf. Abraham was God's prophet and was under his protection, even if Abraham had caused the situation in which he needed God's protection.

We quote Solomon's words again:

> They [Abraham's household] were wandering from nation to nation
> and from one kingdom to another people.
> Yet he did not permit anyone to oppress them.
> He rebuked kings on their account:
> "You must not touch my anointed ones.
> Against my prophets you must do no harm."
> (1 Chronicles 16:20-22)

God Fulfills His Promise: Isaac is born—Genesis 21:1-21

Not long after this, Isaac was born. Isaac means laughter. A year earlier, Sarah had laughed in doubt. Now she was laughing for joy. She said: "God has made me laugh. . . . Who would have said to Abraham that Sarah would nurse children? Yet I have borne a son for him in his old age" (Genesis 21:6-7). There was no doubt that God had performed a miracle. Abraham was a hundred years old, and Sarah had been barren throughout her 90 years. Yet Sarah conceived at the specific time God had said she would. On the eighth day, Abraham circumcised Isaac.

In a believer's life, problems always seem to accompany blessings. Several years later, when Isaac was weaned and Abraham threw a feast for him, Abraham's son Ishmael mocked him. Sarah saw this and reacted in anger. In fact, Sarah reacted like she had 14 years earlier when Hagar became pregnant and mocked her for being barren. At that time, Sarah told Hagar to leave. And now, when Ishmael mocked Isaac, Sarah wanted both of them gone. Ishmael may have thought that since he was the firstborn, it would be easy for him to claim the inheritance after Abraham died. Sarah seems to have gotten that impression: "For the son of this slave will not be heir with my son Isaac," she told Abraham. (Genesis 21:10).

When Abraham resisted Sarah's demand, the Lord told him to do what she wanted, and the Lord comforted him with the fact that Ishmael, too, would grow into a large nation. Yet God wanted there to be no doubt in anyone's mind as to who would be the heir of the promise. At God's command and trusting in God's promise, Abraham did God's bidding. He obediently sent her off "early in the morning," a phrase we'll hear again in a few verses when God commanded him to sacrifice Isaac.

We can just see Abraham's tears when he sent Hagar and Ishmael off into the desert. There, the water ran out. When it was gone, she put some distance between herself and the young man, Ishmael, and prepared to die. But the Angel of God—God himself, who often appeared to people in the Old Testament when they needed deliverance—appeared to her. He had heard Ishmael's prayer and repeated to Hagar the promise that, like Isaac, Ishmael too would become a great nation. After God supplied the two with more water, he gave Ishmael the greatest gift of all: his abiding presence and blessing on Ishmael's life. He grew, and with the wife Hagar got for him in Egypt, God fulfilled that promise.

Abraham in the New Testament

Matthew 1:1,2

[1] A record of the genealogy of Jesus Christ, the son of David, the son of Abraham. [2] Abraham was the father

of Isaac. Isaac was the father of Jacob. Jacob was the father of Judah and his brothers.

Abraham was the physical father of the Jewish nation. All the Jewish people trace their ancestry back to him through Isaac and Jacob. Matthew traced Jesus' ancestry through those three, and then through one of Jacob's sons, Judah.

Galatians 4:21-31

Paul often used something from Abraham's life to establish a truth or to encourage us to act in a certain way. In this case, however, Paul referred to an event in Abraham's life that "can be used as an illustration" (Galatians 4:24). In other words, the event did not take place to teach us a particular truth. But looking back at it, one can use it to illustrate a Scriptural truth.

What Paul said here about Hagar and Ishmael is not meant to label them as unbelievers. Instead, he wanted to make a point using Hagar and Ishmael's circumstances in life—a slave woman and her son born by a human plan—in contrast to Sarah and Isaac's circumstances in life—a free woman and her son born miraculously by God's promise.

> [21] Tell me, you who want to be under the law, are you really listening to the law? [22] For it is written that Abraham had two sons, one by the slave woman, and one by the free woman. [23] However, the son by the slave woman was born according to the flesh, but the son by the free woman was born through a promise. [24] These things can be used as an illustration; namely, the women are two covenants. One is from Mount Sinai, bearing children into slavery. This is Hagar. [25] You see, this Hagar is Mount Sinai in Arabia, and she corresponds to present-day Jerusalem, because Jerusalem is in slavery along with her children. [26] But the Jerusalem

that is above is free. She is our mother. ²⁷ For it is written: "Rejoice, barren woman who does not give birth. Break forth and shout for joy, woman who does not suffer birth pains, because the barren woman has more children than does the woman who has a husband."

²⁸ Now you, brothers, like Isaac, are children of the promise. ²⁹ But just as back then the one who was born according to the flesh persecuted the one who was born according to the Spirit, so this is also the case now. ³⁰ But what does the Scripture say? "Throw out the slave woman and her son, because the son of the slave woman will certainly not receive the inheritance with the son of the free woman." ³¹ For this same reason, brothers, we are not children of a slave woman, but of the free woman.

In verse 21, "the law" refers to two things. First, it refers to the body of laws God gave to Israel through Moses, which is how Paul used it in the phrase "who want to be under the law." Then, it refers to the entire content of the five books of Moses, which is how Paul uses it in the phrase, "are you really listening to the law?"

Some Jewish people to whom Paul was writing wanted to follow the laws God gave Israel through Moses (law in the first sense). But Paul told them to take a careful look at everything written in the Law (law in the second sense), which included the accounts of Hagar and Ishmael and of Sarah and Isaac.

The heart of Christianity is freedom from the Law and the gift of forgiveness, which is what Paul wanted his hearers to have. The essence of human religion is salvation by keeping God's law. Paul used the account of Sarah and Hagar to help his readers see the difference and find their salvation in

Christ alone. To do that, he contrasts "Sarah religion" with "Hagar religion."

Sarah was a free woman, while Hagar was a slave woman. Sarah religion gives freedom while Hagar religion leads to slavery.

In Sarah religion salvation comes according to God's plan—to those who believe in God's promised Savior. In Hagar religion salvation is based on human thinking and planning—to those who do the right things.

Hagar religion and Sarah religion are both based on a covenant. Paul associates Hagar religion with the Law covenant that God gave Israel on Mount Sinai. This Law was good if properly understood and applied. But the Jewish people had misapplied the Law and made it God's way of salvation. So Paul associated Hagar religion with the city of Jerusalem, the headquarters of those who were misapplying the Law in his day and leading Christians away from Christ. Sarah religion is also a religion of those who live in Jerusalem, but not the physical, earthly Jerusalem. Rather, they were citizens of what Paul calls the Jerusalem above, the Jerusalem in Heaven with God. We are there because Christ kept the Law for us.

Sarah religion is miraculous. She was barren, yet she had many, many descendants. Hagar religion—the religion that tries to earn salvation and God's blessing by observing the Law—is of human origin and based on human logic. Her religion would be more popular than Sarah religion. But as foolish as salvation through the cross of Christ might seem, by God's grace, many would find salvation and God's blessing in the cross.

The followers of Hagar religion still persecute the followers of Sarah religion, just like Ishmael persecuted Isaac, thinking he could take Isaac's place as the promised son and father of the great nation God had promised to Abraham. But instead of becoming Abraham's heir, Ishmael and Hagar were forced out of Abraham's family. This teaches us that God wants us to live in the freedom of Sarah religion and never return to the slavery of Hagar religion, no matter how much the world persecutes us for rejecting their way of salvation.

Hebrews 11:11

> [11] By faith Sarah received the ability to conceive children, even though she herself was barren and was past the normal age, because she considered him faithful who made the promise. [12] And so from one man, and he as good as dead, descendants were born as numerous as the stars in the sky and as countless as the sand along the seashore.

Sarah shared Abraham's faith. Although the LORD had to rebuke her weakness, faith in God's promise defined her life, just as it did Abraham's.[25] Faith in God's promise enabled her to be the mother of a great nation along with Abraham.

What we learn about Abraham, Hagar/Ishmael, and Sarah/Isaac from the New Testament: Abraham is considered the father of the Jewish nation. Abraham's son Ishmael can be viewed as a symbol of the Law covenant, which holds people in

---

[25] You may be using a version in which the writer is said to be describing Abraham's faith, not Sarah's. There are a few reasons why some translators think the verse is talking about Abraham's faith (or both Abraham's faith and Sarah's faith). The Greek text has "Sarah" as the subject, not "Abraham." Note that the NIV84 adds Abraham and makes both him and Sarah the subjects. However, the NIV11 changed that and has Sarah alone as the subject.

slavery. Isaac is a symbol of the Gospel covenant of forgiveness, which gives freedom. Also, we dare not forget about Sarah's faith in God's promises. Through faith she would bear the son who would be the heir of the promises God gave to Abraham.

The Life of Abraham

Abraham Meets Abimelek, Part Two—21:22-34

Sometime after Isaac was weaned, Abimelek and the commander of his army, Phicol, came to Abraham to solidify their relationship. Note the depth of Abimelek's faith and understanding. He took seriously what God had said about Abraham's greatness. He asked Abraham to deal kindly with him and everyone else in the surrounding area. Abraham promised that he would.

A little later, Abimelek's servants took control of one of Abraham's wells. Rather than being a source of contention between Abimelek and Abraham, this situation led to a formal treaty between them. As part of the treaty, Abraham gave Abimelek seven lambs, and Abimelek's acceptance of them was his testimony that the well belonged to Abraham. They named the place Beersheba.[26]

At Beersheba, Abraham found a wonderful place to raise his son, Isaac. They could live among people who knew the true God, respected Abraham as God's prophet, and were eager to live in harmony with him. Out of thanks to the Lord, Abraham prepared a place of worship. He called on the name

---

[26] The EHV note on this verse reads, "Beersheba can mean *well of the oath* or *well of seven*." In either case, it refers to the existence of peace between Abraham and the residents of the land.

of the LORD and honored him as the true and faithful God who existed from eternity past to eternity future.

The Conversation

Eliezar and Phicol are real people, engaged in a fictional conversation with Caleb and Merit. The characters reflect on the good things they have experienced by being with Abraham—even though Abraham's sin was partly instrumental in bringing those things about. The characters:

Eliezar: Abraham's chief steward.

Caleb: One of Abraham's servants and a mature believer in the true God.

Phicol: The commander of Abimelek's army.

Merit: One of the servants Pharaoh gave to Abraham.

> *Phicol:* May I say something?
>
> *Eliezar:* Of course, Phicol.
>
> *Phicol:* Abraham was wrong to deceive us. He caused us a lot of pain. I can't understand why he did that, especially since he had God's promise that God would give him a son within the year. And Abraham believed that promise. He must have thought we were a bunch of idol worshippers with no sense of right and wrong.
>
> *Caleb:* We've been all over that, Phicol. We're not standing behind what Abraham did. . . .
>
> *Phicol* interrupting: Caleb, that's not where I'm going. What I'm getting at is how blessed I feel. Sure, Abraham was wrong. But look how it all turned out. Abimelek and many of us knew about the true God, and

we believed in him. We knew about God's promise of a Savior. But we had no idea of the far-reaching promises God had made to Abraham. We thought, . . . well, we didn't know what to think about him. Maybe he was just a squatter, or a rich nomad thinking of taking our land. But we never imagined that he was a prophet of God. But now we know. And he has invited us to his worship services. Now we can listen to God speaking to us. After all, we are one of the nations that will be blessed through Abraham.

Merit: I agree with everything Phicol just said. I went through the same thing, and it was hard to leave Egypt. But I wouldn't want it any other way. I know that God has blessed me too. All I knew were the gods of Egypt. But now I know the true God, and every year I live with these people, I learn more about him. My family feels the same way.

Eliezar: You speak with a fine spirit, Phicol . . . and you too, Merit. Phicol, if our servants have any more disagreements, I know we can come to you and Abimelek. Abraham is often afraid of what the people of the land might do. But he'll feel safe living here, and he and Sarah will feel safe raising Isaac with you close by.

Closing

As you read this response, focus on God's fulfillment of his promise of a Savior. Like Israel, we praise God for what he accomplished through Jesus.

Isaiah 29:18-24

On that day, the deaf will hear the words from a book,

and out of gloom and darkness the eyes of the
    blind will see.
The humble will rejoice in the Lord once again,
    and the poor will delight in the Holy One of Israel.
But the ruthless will come to nothing
    and all those who plan evil will be cut off—
Therefore this is what the Lord, who redeemed Abraham, says about the house of Jacob:
Jacob will not be ashamed anymore.
His face will not grow pale.
But when his children see what I do among them,
    they will honor my name.
They will honor the Holy One of Jacob.
They will stand in awe of the God of Israel.
Those who are confused will come to understand,
    and those who complain will gladly receive
        instruction.

Chapter 9
Genesis 22

God Tests Abraham—22:1-14
God Renews His Promise to Abraham—22:15-19

Prayer: Dear heavenly Father, give me the same confidence Abraham had, namely, that you have provided a Lamb as a sacrifice in my place. Inspire me by Abraham's trust in you and his confidence in your promises. Help me serve and obey you in my life, even as I trust in your gift of salvation. Amen.

The Life of Abraham

God Tests Abraham—22:1-14

In this lesson, we will see Abraham's personal righteousness, that is, his obedience when God commanded him to do something very difficult. After we look at this account, we will come back to the keyword, righteousness.

This wonderful account gets us to the heart of our lives of faith as God's people. It points us to our Savior and his sacrifice for us.

God told Abraham to sacrifice Isaac. The way God told him to do this almost sounds cruel: "Now take your son, *your only son, whom you love,* Isaac, and go to the land of Moriah. Offer him there as a burnt offering on one of the mountains there, the one to which I direct you" (Genesis 22:2). Abraham had waited so long for Isaac. He was Abraham and Sarah's only son, and he loved him dearly. But this was a test, and God's intent was to make it as hard as possible.

Abraham did as God commanded. Early in the morning, he gathered what he needed to sacrifice Isaac. He chose two of his servants and headed north to where God directed him. Abraham came to the land of Moriah, a place that plays a significant role in God's fulfillment of his promise of a Savior.

Isaac wondered where his father would get the lamb for the sacrifice. Abraham told him, "God himself will provide the lamb for a burnt offering, my son" (Genesis 22:8). Humanly speaking, God's command would destroy the promise. But Abraham obeyed God.

When they arrived at the mountain in the region of Moriah to which God had directed him, Abraham built an altar, arranged the wood, tied up Isaac, and placed him on the altar. We note that Isaac, who at this time was in his teenage years, could probably have escaped his father's grasp. But he didn't put up a fight. He was content to follow God's will.

Finally, at the point when Abraham raised the knife to kill Isaac, God put a stop to the test. The Angel of the LORD appeared, God himself, the messenger whom God often sent in the Old Testament to help his people, and he told Abraham to stop. Then he provided a ram as a sacrifice in Isaac's place.

Abraham's response to Isaac's earlier question came true. He had told Isaac, "God himself will provide the lamb for a burnt offering, my son" (Genesis 22:8). God did provide a

CHAPTER 9   Genesis 22

substitute for Isaac, and Abraham offered the ram in Isaac's place.

Abraham gave the mountain a new name, Jehovah-Jireh, which means "The LORD sees." God provided the sacrifice. From that a saying arose: *"On the mountain of the LORD it will be provided."*[27]

From the beginning of the test, God had pointed Abraham in the direction of Mount Moriah. This was a special place. It was just outside the city of Salem, where Abraham had met Melchizedek many years before.[28] It was where Solomon built a temple to the Lord, where the sacrifices that pictured Jesus, the Lamb of God, would be offered. And it was where

---

[27] In verse 7, Isaac had asked his father about the lamb they were to sacrifice to the Lord. Abraham replied that "God sees for himself." After the sacrifice, a saying arose: "On the mountain of the LORD he sees." Since Isaac wondered who would provide a sacrificial lamb, most translations translate "see" as "provide." We might think of it this way. Abraham to Isaac: God himself sees the need for a sacrifice, and he will provide one. God to us: I've seen your need for a sacrifice for sin, and I have provided one.

[28] In Samuel's day, the ark of the Lord had been removed from the tabernacle that the Israelites had made in the wilderness before they conquered the Promised Land. It had been captured by the Philistines in a battle, and they soon returned it. For some twenty years it was stored in Kiriath-jearim. When King David captured the city of Jerusalem and made it his capital, he wanted to bring the ark into the city, where he had decided to put it in a permanent temple he was planning to build. The ark never made it into the city. It was temporarily stored outside the city on a threshing floor. That threshing floor became incorporated into the city of Jerusalem. It was on that threshing floor that David's son Solomon built the temple: "Then Solomon began to build the House of the LORD at Jerusalem on Mount Moriah, where the LORD had appeared to his father David. He constructed it on the site that David had specified, namely, the threshing floor of Ornan the Jebusite" (2 Chronicles 3:1). It was near there, right outside the city of Jerusalem, that God provided a sacrifice for us.

Jesus died as our substitute. The saying expressed the Old Testament believers' faith in God's promise of a Savior.

From this we see that Abraham and his descendants did not merely think of their sacrifices as gifts to God. They realized that their sacrifices also pictured God's gift to them—the sacrifice God would offer for their sins. Note the phrase, "to this day." This refers to the day when Moses wrote this account. The truth that God would provide a sacrifice for sin originated long before Moses' day; it was known in Abraham's day. The fact that Abraham shared the righteousness that comes by faith with believers before him, like Noah (Hebrews 11:7), shows that believers from Adam on down understood God's promise in the same way.

God Renews His Promise to Abraham—22:15-19

In this account of Abraham and Isaac, God saw that Abraham's faith and love for him were genuine. Abraham had sacrificed Isaac in his heart. Because of this, God appeared to Abraham and said, "Now I know that you fear God" (Genesis 22:12).

After Abraham sacrificed the ram God provided, God appeared to Abraham a second time and affirmed his promise to bless all nations through him. Reread Genesis 22:15-18 below. As you do, look for the reason why God took an oath to fulfill his Gospel promise through Abraham:

> The Angel of the LORD called to Abraham a second time from heaven [16] and said, "I have sworn by myself, declares the LORD, because you have done this thing and have not withheld your son, your only son, I will bless you greatly, and I will multiply your descendants greatly, like the stars of the sky and like the sand on the

seashore. Your descendants will take possession of the city gates of their enemies. In your seed all the nations of the earth will be blessed, because you have obeyed my voice." (Genesis 22:15-18).

In these verses, God twice based his blessing on Abraham's acts of faith, 1) because Abraham had "not withheld his son" (verse 16); and (2) because Abraham had obeyed God's voice (verse 18). Twice God used the word "because." In Hebrew, the word "because" gives the reason why someone does something, just like it does in English. Here God told Abraham that he would bless him "because" Abraham obeyed him and was willing to give up his son Isaac, whom he had long awaited.

Keyword: "Righteousness"
Part Four, A Christian's Righteousness

We have already considered the word righteousness three times. First, God was acting righteously when he continued to fulfill his promise of a Savior when he called Abraham to play a major role in its fulfillment. Second, we saw a man named Melchizedek, whose name means "king of righteousness." Melchizedek was a picture of Christ, *the* King of Righteousness. He was a picture of the Savior who would win the righteousness we need to become God's children. Third, faith in God's promise of the son from whom the Savior would come was credited to Abraham as righteousness, just like our faith in Christ is credited to us as righteousness.

In the account of Abraham's willingness to sacrifice his son, we see a fourth aspect of righteousness. This is the righteousness that believers produce in their lives because we know we are righteous in Christ. Our righteousness is never perfect, and it is not the reason why we are saved. However, when God looks at our righteousness, he says he will bless us *because* of it (Genesis 15:15-18).[29]

In Abraham's case, we know that God did not declare Abraham righteous because he sacrificed his son. God had already declared Abraham righteous through faith in his promise (Genesis 15:6). What is more, Abraham's obedience did not make the promise more certain. God made the promise absolutely certain by swearing on himself to fulfill it (Genesis 22:16). That is what made the promise certain for Abraham and for us. The writer of Hebrews makes a special point of that, as we will see.

Even so, God told Abraham that he would bless him *"because you have obeyed my voice"* (Genesis 22:18). What exactly does that mean? Did Abraham's obedience make it more certain that God would fulfill the promise he had given him twenty-five years earlier? Did the gift of righteousness God had given Abraham by faith become greater or more pure

---

[29] Note two other passages of Scripture that point to Abraham's works as the basis for the blessings God gave him. When God repeated his promises to Abraham's son Isaac, he again linked those promises to Abraham's faith: "I will multiply your offspring as the stars of heaven and will give to your offspring all these lands. And in your offspring all the nations of the earth shall be blessed, because Abraham obeyed my voice and kept my charge, my commandments, my statutes, and my laws" (Genesis 26:4-5). Nehemiah also referred to Abraham's works of faith: "You found his heart to be faithful before you. You made the covenant with him to give to his descendants the land of the Canaanites, the Hittites, the Amorites and the Perizzites, and the Jebusites and the Girgashites. You kept your word, because you are righteous" (Nehemiah 9:7,8). God blessed Abraham *because of* Abraham's faithfulness, but the blessing had its origin in God's own righteousness.

because Abraham obeyed God more? Did God's oath get a boost because of Abraham's righteousness? No.

But many have answered these questions with yes. And they live with a focus on their own obedience, becoming more certain of God's promises the more obedient they become.

A careful reading of those passages, however, shows that this interpretation is wrong. If so, what does it mean that God would bless Abraham because Abraham had obeyed him? In other words, what role did Abraham's obedience play in his receiving God's blessing?

Let's look at Genesis 22:11-18 where God linked his blessings with Abraham's obedience to him.

Then we will look at other places in Scripture that link God's blessings to the good works we do in obedience to him. These other passages will help us understand why God affirmed his promise to Abraham by saying to him, "*because you have obeyed my voice.*"

Genesis 22:11-18

When God spoke to Abraham after Abraham had obeyed him, God said nothing about declaring Abraham righteous (or justifying him). James speaks that way, but Moses doesn't. Moses uses other equivalent ways of speaking, however. When the Angel of the Lord first spoke to Abraham, he said, "Do not lay your hand on the boy. Do not do anything to him. For now I know that you fear God, because you have not withheld your son, your only son, from me" (Genesis 22:12). The Lord here said that Abraham's obedience proved that Abraham feared him, that is, he loved and respected him.

The second time the L㎞ORD spoke to Abraham, he said that because Abraham obeyed him, he would shower on him the blessings he had promised him earlier. One of those blessings was that in Abraham and his seed all the nations of the earth would be blessed. (We previously saw that Paul called this blessing the gospel message and that the "seed" referred to Christ.) Again, we are not told that God declared Abraham righteous because of his obedience. Rather, we are told that Abraham's obedience assured him that God would fulfill his gospel promise *through him, Abraham.*

Neither of these statements specifically says that God declared Abraham righteous by what he did. God had already declared Abraham righteous through faith (Genesis 15:6). As we will see below, James interprets the Lord's words to Abraham as saying that, and rightly so.

Before we look at what James says about this event in Abraham's life, let's look at what the writer of Hebrews says about an event in these verses.

The writer says,

> [13] For God made a promise to Abraham, and since God had no one greater to swear by, "He swore by himself." [14] He said, "I will most certainly bless you and make you increase in number." [15] And so in this way, after Abraham had waited patiently, he received the promise.
>
> [16] To be sure, people swear by someone who is greater, and the oath serves as a confirmation for them that ends all disputes. [17] Because God wanted to show the heirs of the promise with even greater certainty that his plan was unchangeable, he guaranteed his promise with an oath. [18] He did this so that, through two unchangeable things (in which it is impossible that God would lie), we, who have fled for refuge by taking hold of this

hope that is held out to us, might have strong encouragement.

[19] We have this hope as an anchor for the soul. It is sure and firm, and it goes behind the inner curtain, [20] where Jesus entered ahead of us on our behalf, because he became a high priest forever like Melchizedek. (Hebrews 6:13-20).

In the same account where God said he would bless Abraham because Abraham obeyed him, God made his promise certain to Abraham (and to us) by swearing an oath on himself.

The writer of Hebrews makes it completely clear that this oath made the promise certain. Abraham received the promise "because he waited patiently" (6:15), not because he obeyed God. God made this oath to guarantee that "his plan was unchangeable" (6:17). He did this so that we "might have strong encouragement" (6:18). This oath assured that God's promise of a Savior is "sure and firm" (6:19). In fact, there is no mention of Abraham's obedience and that it made God's promise more certain for himself or for anyone else.

Again we note that this is in the same account that James uses to show that Abraham's faith justified him. Let's now look at what James says and interpret it in light of God wanting to make his promise certain by swearing an oath on himself.

James 2:20-24

This is perhaps the most well-known example of how Scripture links good works and salvation, and the one most regularly discussed in Bible classes. The key to interpreting this verse is found in the context. James was writing to people who claimed that one's lack of personal righteousness bears no relation to God declaring them righteous in Christ (or justifying them). James replied that on the contrary, it does. He wrote,

> [14] What good is it, my brothers, if a man claims to have faith but has no deeds? Can such faith save him? [15] Suppose a brother or sister is without clothes and daily food. [16] If one of you says to him, "Go, I wish you well; keep warm and well fed," but does nothing about his physical needs, what good is it? [17] In the same way, faith by itself, if it is not accompanied by action, is dead. (James 2:14-17 NIV84)

James called faith that is not accompanied by works of service to God a dead faith—in other words, no faith at all. He continued

> [18] But someone will say, "You have faith; I have deeds." Show me your faith without deeds, and I will show you my faith by what I do. [19] You believe that there is one God. Good! Even the demons believe that—and shudder. [20] You foolish man, do you want evidence that faith without deeds is useless? (James 2:18-20 NIV84)

The people to whom James was writing might say, "I have faith. I am saved by faith alone. Deeds, whether they are good or bad, have no place in my Christianity." James did not deny that his detractors had faith. But what kind of faith did they have if it was devoid of works. James had called it "such faith" (2:14). After all, even the demons have faith that God exists. Yet their faith does not lead them to serve God; it only makes them shudder. Those who have some sort of faith but not faith in Christ as their Savior have a faith that is useless both for their own salvation and for the welfare of others. They have not been declared righteous. Their faith is either dead or it is not Christian faith.

James now gives two examples of living faith: that of Abraham and of Rahab. In both cases, their works showed that they had faith. But notice that James puts it a little differently. He says that because a believer's faith leads to good works, their faith is now complete. It is now the faith through which they have been declared righteous and has made them pleasing to God. This is a much more forceful way of putting it.

This statement has led many to think that they are saved *both* by faith and by works. This is wrong. Such thoughts always lead us back to what Paul said in Romans 3: "For we conclude that a person is justified by faith without the works of the law" (Romans 3:8). These words express the foundation of the Christian religion: we are righteous by faith alone through Christ alone.

But note what Paul himself had written a few verses earlier: "For it is not those who hear the law who are righteous in God's sight, but it is those who obey the law who will be declared righteous" (Romans 2:13 NIV84). Note the phrase: *"those who do the law . . . will be declared righteous."* Here Paul was addressing people who knew the Law but who were not keeping it, the same people to whom James was writing. And he was speaking just like James was.

James uses Abraham and Rahab to make the point Paul was making in Romans 2:13

> [21] Was not our ancestor Abraham considered righteous for what he did when he offered his son Isaac on the altar? [22] You see that his faith and his actions were working together, and his faith was made complete by what he did. [23] And the scripture was fulfilled that says, "Abraham believed God, and it was credited to him as righteousness," and he was called God's friend. [24] You

see that a person is justified by what he does and not by faith alone. (James 2:21-24)

Abraham believed that God would use Isaac to fulfill his promise of a Savior, and for that reason, God credited it to him as righteousness. At the same time, he did what God wanted him to do. And James, speaking in terms of what some of his readers were denying, said God considered him righteous for that reason.

James said the same thing about Rahab's works:

> ^{25} In the same way, was not even Rahab the prostitute considered righteous for what she did when she gave lodging to the spies and sent them off in a different direction? ^{26} As the body without the spirit is dead, so faith without deeds is dead. (James 2:25,26 NIV84)

Rahab was a prostitute who lived in Jericho when the Israelites were ready to occupy the Promised Land. She knew God's promise to the Israelites and believed that God would destroy Jericho (Joshua 2:8-13). Her faith was made complete when she kept the Israelite spies from being captured. She too was considered righteous because her faith was coupled with her works.

After James used Rahab to make his point, he repeated what he said in verse 17: "For just as the body without breath is dead, so also faith without works is dead" (James 2:26).

Returning to the account of Abraham in Genesis 22, we read that when Abraham obeyed God by giving up his son Isaac, God said to him, "*Now* I know that you fear God, because you have not withheld your son, your only son, from me" (Genesis 22:12). We understand what that means. Abraham feared God long before this, and God certainly knew that he did. But at this point, when God said, "*Now* I know that you fear God," he was responding to Abraham's obedience in the greatest test of his life. Abraham's faith was made complete by his works in a remarkable way.

James describes Abraham's relationship with God in another way, that of friendship. When Abraham obeyed the Lord, the Scripture was fulfilled that said he was God's friend. We don't hear about this in Genesis, but we do in two other places in Scripture. The believing king, Jehoshaphat, prayed, "Was it not you, our God, who drove out the inhabitants of this land in front of your people Israel? You gave it to the descendants of your friend Abraham forever" (2 Chronicles 20:7). And God said something similar through the prophet Isaiah,

> [8] But you, O Israel, my servant,
> O Jacob, whom I have chosen,
> the offspring of Abraham, whom I love,
> [9] whom I have snatched from the ends of the earth,
> whom I have called from its corners....
> (Isaiah 41:8,9)

When you add all these things together, (1) that God had declared Abraham righteous long before the account in Genesis 22, (2) that Abraham was certain of God's promise because of God's oath to fulfill it, not because he had obeyed God, (3) that God swore on himself to fulfill the promise at the same time he said that Abraham would inherit the promised blessings *because* he had obeyed God, (4) because James gives us the specific context in which he said that we are declared righteous by our deeds in addition to faith, and (5) that Paul himself, who insisted in all his letters that we are saved by faith in Christ alone, could also say "it is those who obey the law who will be declared righteous" (Romans 2:13)—all of this shows that James is not saying that good works are necessary for salvation. Rather, he is saying that *good works are necessary*, as the Lutheran Confessions puts it. We are saved through faith alone. But Scripture is clear: The faith by which we are saved—by which we are declared righteous—is never alone.

We continue with other passages in Scripture that say God blesses us on the basis of what we do for him.

John 15:10

> [10] If you keep my commandments, you will abide in my love, just as I have kept my Father's commandments and abide in his love.

Jesus kept every command his Father gave him. Because of this, he remained in his Father's love. The same is true for us. If we seek to follow God's will, it's because we love him as he loves us, and if we do his will we will remain in his love. The verse can easily be understood if we express it the other way around: Rejecting God's commandments and rebelling against his will means rejecting his love for us and cutting ourselves off from his love.

John 14:21

> [21] Whoever has my commandments and keeps them, he it is who loves me. And he who loves me will be loved by my Father, and I will love him and manifest myself to him.

This verse also links our works with God's love for us. If we keep God's commandments, it's because we love Jesus. If we love Jesus, we will be loved by his Father, and Jesus will show himself to us.

Matthew 25:20-21

> And he who had received the five talents came forward, bringing five talents more, saying, "Master, you delivered to me five talents; here, I have made five talents more." His master said to him, "Well done, good and faithful servant. You have been faithful over a little; I will set you over much. Enter into the joy of your master."

Jesus here described what will happen at the final judgment. He urged us always to be about his business and to use the wealth he has given us wisely. To those who *do this*, he will say, "Well done, good and faithful servant. . . . Enter into the joy of your master." Every Christian wants to hear those words, and we take Jesus' encouragement to serve him seriously.

Matthew 25:31-46

This principle comes out clearly in Jesus' account of Judgment Day.

> [31] When the Son of Man comes in his glory, and all the angels with him, then he will sit on his glorious throne. [32] Before him will be gathered all the nations, and he will separate people one from another as a shepherd separates the sheep from the goats. [33] And he will place the sheep on his right, but the goats on the left.
>
> [34] Then the King will say to those on his right, "Come, you who are blessed by my Father, inherit the kingdom prepared for you from the foundation of the world. [35] For I was hungry and you gave me food, I was thirsty and you gave me drink, I was a stranger and you welcomed me, [36] I was naked and you clothed me, I was sick and you visited me, I was in prison and you came to me." [37] Then the righteous will answer him, saying,

"Lord, when did we see you hungry and feed you, or thirsty and give you drink? ³⁸ And when did we see you a stranger and welcome you, or naked and clothe you? ³⁹ And when did we see you sick or in prison and visit you?" ⁴⁰ And the King will answer them, "Truly, I say to you, as you did it to one of the least of these my brothers, you did it to me."

⁴¹ "Then he will say to those on his left, 'Depart from me, you cursed, into the eternal fire prepared for the devil and his angels. ⁴² For I was hungry and you gave me no food, I was thirsty and you gave me no drink, ⁴³ I was a stranger and you did not welcome me, naked and you did not clothe me, sick and in prison and you did not visit me.' ⁴⁴ Then they also will answer, saying, "Lord, when did we see you hungry or thirsty or a stranger or naked or sick or in prison, and did not minister to you?"

⁴⁵ Then he will answer them, saying, "Truly, I say to you, as you did not do it to one of the least of these, you did not do it to me."

⁴⁶ And these will go away into eternal punishment, but the righteous into eternal life.

In these verses, Jesus does not have in mind the general good works people do, like helping the poor or doing deeds of kindness to those who are suffering. Those works are certainly good, and Christians do them out of love for others.

Jesus has another kind of good works in mind. He is referring to things Christians do as Christians—things we do *for him*. Note that the examples Jesus uses are works of service Christians do for fellow Christians who are being persecuted. Christians go out on a limb to befriend fellow Christians who need their help and support by giving them food, clothing, shelter, and even visiting them in prison. We are fully aware that our acts of service might cause us to be persecuted as well, that we might land in the same prison cell in which those we are visiting are confined.

On the last day, Jesus says, believers will wonder when they actually saw Jesus and served him. Jesus will answer that whenever they served "the least of these brothers of mine," they were serving him (Matthew 25:40).

This becomes even clearer when the unbelievers ask Jesus when they saw him and refused to serve him. After all, some of them probably did more philanthropic works of charity than many Christians do. The problem is, Jesus said, that they weren't serving *him*. In fact, they *couldn't* serve him because they couldn't recognize him in his followers.

This account is as much about faith as it is about good works. Jesus says that he will judge believers on the basis of the good things they did out of love for him. Jesus was not teaching salvation by works any more than James was. Rather, he was pointing to the faith-generated works Christians did—to their *"faith working through love"* (Galatians 5:6). And he was pointing to the unbeliever's lack of such works. They couldn't do the works he lists because they neither knew him nor had concern for "the least of these my brothers."

Romans 2:6-11

Paul described Judgment Day in terms of what people do in their lives.

> [6] He will render to each one according to his works: [7] to those who by patience in well-doing seek for glory and honor and immortality, he will give eternal life; [8] but for those who are self-seeking and do not obey the truth, but obey unrighteousness, there will be wrath

and fury. ⁹ There will be tribulation and distress for every human being who does evil, the Jew first and also the Greek, ¹⁰ but glory and honor and peace for everyone who does good, the Jew first and also the Greek. ¹¹ For God shows no partiality.

The first part of the book of Romans, leading up to Romans 3:21, is primarily Law. Paul is teaching that God does not show favoritism and that he will judge impartially.

In these verses, Paul described the life of a believer and that of an unbeliever. He could have said that God will judge each person on the basis of their faith or lack of it. Rather, he says that God will judge each person according to what their lives were like.

Paul says the same thing in 2 Corinthians 5:10: "For we must all appear before the judgment seat of Christ, so that each one may receive what is due for what he has done in the body, whether good or evil." Statements like this don't make Christians afraid. Rather, they make us think hard about our lives and ask God to make us more fruitful in serving him. And they set us at peace when we see ourselves serving God in love.

1 John 4:16–21

> ¹⁶ We also have come to know and trust the love that God has for us.
>
> God is love. Whoever remains in love remains in God and God in him. ¹⁷ In this way his love has been brought to its goal among us, so that we may have confidence on the day of judgment, because in this world we are just like Jesus. ¹⁸ There is no fear in love, but complete love drives out fear, because fear has to do

with punishment. The one who continues to be afraid has not been brought to the goal in love.

[19] We love because he first loved us. [20] If anyone says, "I love God," but hates his brother, he is a liar. For how can anyone who does not love his brother, whom he has seen, love God, whom he has not seen? [21] This then is the command we have from him: The one who loves God should also love his brother.

How can we be confident to face the judgement? The normal answer is "because we are forgiven in Christ." What drives fear out of our hearts? The normal answer is "because of God's perfect love for us." This is true. But does John say that here?

Here's how George Stoeckhardt[30] interprets this passage:

> This is said of the love that is with us, that dwells in us. It is our love, which has its origin in God. This love has reached its end and purpose when it enables us to face Judgment Day with confidence. By this everyone can test himself whether he really possesses this love, as he considers in what frame of mind he approaches Judgment Day. Whoever has this God-born love is not frightened at the thought of Judgment Day. He approaches this Day with fearless confidence. He enters the presence of the great Judge unafraid.
>
> ... We must remember that the Apostle at this place does not say how Christians, terrified about their sins, should meet the thought of Judgment Day. Only by faith in Christ, which apprehends the merits of Christ, can one stand before the Judge. That is here presupposed. From such faith necessarily flows love. That faith

---

[30] George Stoeckhardt taught Bible interpretation at Concordia Seminary from 1878 to 1913. He was the Missouri Synod's first exegete, working together with C. F. W. Walther. The two were close co-workers.

in Christ quiets our heart against sin, we have read earlier in this epistle. Yet what the Apostle writes here is meant to test our faith. Are we terrified by the thought of Judgment! We ought not be. Our love is an evidence of faith.[31]

Such an interpretation does justice to John's words. Of course we will rest on Jesus' forgiveness on the last day. But here John is directing our attention to the fruits of our faith in God's forgiveness in Christ. Those fruits will also bring us comfort on the last day when we hear Jesus say to us, "Well done, good and faithful servant! . . . Enter into the joy of your master" (Matthew 25:21).

Romans 8:11-14

> [11] If the Spirit of him who raised Jesus from the dead dwells in you, he who raised Christ Jesus from the dead will also give life to your mortal bodies through his Spirit who dwells in you. [12] So then, brothers, we are debtors, not to the flesh, to live according to the flesh. [13] For if you live according to the flesh you will die, but if by the Spirit you put to death the deeds of the body, you will live. [14] For all who are led by the Spirit of God are sons of God.

Here again, Paul links our deeds to God's verdict on the last day. If we put to death the deeds of the body, we will live. Jesus has raised us from death and given us the Spirit of life. The Spirit enables us to put to death the misdeeds of the sinful nature. If he is doing this in us, we are children of God.

Paul says something similar in Galatians, "I have been crucified with Christ. It is no longer I who live, but Christ who lives in me" (Galatians 2:20).

---

[31] George Stoeckhardt, *Lectures on the Three Letters of John*, tr. H.W. Degner (Aitkin, MN: Hope Press, 1963), pp. 108,109.

Matthew 5:17-20

> [17] Do not think that I have come to abolish the Law or the Prophets; I have not come to abolish them but to fulfill them. [18] For truly, I say to you, until heaven and earth pass away, not an iota, not a dot, will pass from the Law until all is accomplished. [19] Therefore whoever relaxes one of the least of these commandments and teaches others to do the same will be called least in the kingdom of heaven, but whoever does them and teaches them will be called great in the kingdom of heaven. [20] For I tell you, unless your righteousness exceeds that of the scribes and Pharisees, you will never enter the kingdom of heaven.

Jesus kept the entire Law for us. His righteousness has become our righteousness. And so, because we are righteous in Christ, we can look at the Law in a new way. We are not like the Pharisees, who had to water down the Law so they could actually keep it. Instead, we can be serious about the smallest detail of the Law because, unlike the Pharisees, we know that God forgives us.

Because we are righteous in Christ, we can strive to keep the Law with our entire heart, soul, and mind. We can do this because we know he will always forgive us when we come up short. This makes our righteousness—our life of righteous living—better than that of the Pharisees. And for this reason, we can be sure that the kingdom of Heaven is ours.

Mathew 6:12,14,15

> [12] Forgive us our debts, as we also forgive our debtors. [14] Indeed, if you forgive people when they sin against you, your heavenly Father will also forgive you. [15] But if you

do not forgive people their sins, your Father will not forgive your sins.

If we forgive others, God will forgive us. And if we don't forgive others, God will not forgive us. This petition of the Lord's Prayer can easily be used to teach work-righteousness. However, if we refuse to forgive others, we have given up any appreciation of God's forgiveness and we have lost our faith. But if we forgive others, we do so because we are living under God's forgiveness, appreciate what God is doing for us, and are compelled to do the same for those who sin against us.

1 Corinthians 15:56-58

> [56] The sting of death is sin, and the power of sin is the law. [57] But thanks be to God, who gives us the victory through our Lord Jesus Christ! [58] Therefore, my dear brothers, be steadfast, immovable, always abounding in the Lord's work, because you know that your labor is not in vain in the Lord.

We are not saved by what we do. Nevertheless, the good things we do for Christ are not done in vain. God will reward us for what we have done. We can even say that he will judge us based on what we have done, like Jesus did in the parable of the sheep and the goats.

Isaiah 64:6

We close this section with a few thoughts on Isaiah 64:6: "All of us have become like something unclean, and all our righteous acts are like a filthy cloth." (or as it is rendered in the NIV11, "and all our righteous acts are like filthy rags.")

In view of everything we have seen about a Christian's good deeds, is it right for us to apply those words to Christians? Let's read this verse in context:

> ⁴ From ancient times no one has heard.
> No ear has understood.
> No eye has seen any god except you,
> who goes into action for the one who waits for him.
> ⁵ You meet anyone who joyfully practices righteousness,
> who remembers you by walking in your ways!
> But you were angry because we sinned.
> We have remained in our sins for a long time.
> Can we still be saved?
> ⁶ All of us have become like something unclean,
> and all our righteous acts are like a filthy cloth.
> All of us have withered like a leaf,
> and our guilt carries us away like the wind.
> ⁷ There is no one who calls on your name,
> who rouses himself to take hold of you.
> So you hid your face from us.
> You made us melt by the power of our guilt.
> ⁸ But now, LORD, you are our father.
> We are the clay, and you are our potter.
> All of us are the work of your hand.
> ⁹ Do not be angry, LORD, without limit.
> Do not remember our guilt forever.
> Please look closely.
> All of us are your people.
> (Isaiah 64:4-9)

In the first verse and a half, Isaiah spoke about God's favor on the person "who joyfully practices righteousness." But then he described Israel's current state. They have remained in their sins for a long time. Their guilt carries them away. No one calls on God's name. God has hid his face from them and made them melt by the power of their guilt. They were unclean and that their righteous acts were like filthy rags.

In other words, they may still have been sacrificing to God and doing other acts required by the law. But there was no fear of God behind those acts. God considered them to be filthy rags. Finally, in the last two verses, Isaiah asked God to return to them and forgive their guilt.

It is argued that since Isaiah said, "all *our* righteous acts," he was saying that his own spiritual life was the same as that of the Israelites around him. If we accept that argument, we must say that Isaiah was unclean, swept away by his sins, had no desire to lay hold of God, and that his righteous deeds were like filthy rags in God's sight. What is more, these words apply to all believers today.

But the prophets often put themselves among God's people even when testifying against their rebellion and sin. For example, after reading the book of Jeremiah and learning that Judah's captivity would soon be over, Daniel made this heartfelt prayer:

> [4] I prayed to the Lord my God and made confession, saying . . . [5] we have sinned and done wrong and acted wickedly and rebelled, turning aside from your commandments. . . . [6] We have not listened to your servants the prophets, who spoke in your name to our kings, our princes, and our fathers, and to all the people of the land. [7] To you, O Lord, belongs righteousness, but to us open shame, as at this day, to the men of Judah, to the inhabitants of Jerusalem, and to all Israel, those who are near and those who are far away, in all the lands to which you have driven them, because of the treachery that they have committed against you. [8] To us, O Lord, belongs open shame, to our kings, to our princes, and to our fathers, because we have sinned against you. [9] To the Lord our God belong mercy and forgiveness, for we have rebelled against him. [10] and have not obeyed

the voice of the L ORD our God by walking in his laws, which he set before us by his servants the prophets. (Daniel 9:4-10)

In these verses, Daniel includes himself in the nation of Israel. But is he including himself in his description of their sins and rebellion? He had just finished reading from the book of Jeremiah. The angel had just addressed him with the words, "Daniel, you are a highly valued man." Then the angel assured him, "Do not be afraid, Daniel, because from the first day that you began to commit your heart to gaining understanding and to humbling yourself before your God, your words have been heard, and I have come in response to your words" (Daniel 10:11-12).

Daniel, like Isaiah, was not describing himself, but in a humble spirit he was praying to God on behalf of the people of Judah, going so far as to include himself in his confession of their sins.

The Reformers used this verse to counter the Catholics, who claimed that we are saved by faith and by works. The Reformers were naturally motivated to point out that good works played no role in salvation as the Catholics claimed. There are many places in Scripture that make that clear. But to tell believers that their good deeds are filthy rags undermines—we might say "destroys"—our efforts to motivate fellow believers and ourselves to become righteous in their own lives as they are in Christ.

The writer of Hebrews encourages us: "Let us also consider carefully how to spur each other on to love and good works" (Hebrews 10:24). It is incongruous at the same time to call those works "filthy rags."

Summary

This entire discussion was aimed at helping us understand why God said to Abraham, "In your seed all the nations of the earth will be blessed, *because you have obeyed my voice*" (Genesis 22:18). Abraham didn't earn the right to be blessed by God. But God assured him of those blessings when he saw Abraham's faith exhibited in his willingness to sacrifice his son, doing so simply because that's what God wanted him to do. In the interest of preserving justification by faith alone, we rightly downplay our good works. However, we dare never downplay the importance of our good works or shirk from saying that God blesses us *because* of them. This is what God said to Abraham.

Properly understood, this way of speaking impresses on us that good works are not just an evidence of our faith. They are what Christians, who know the love of God in Christ, cannot help but do. Christians who humbly trust in God's forgiveness for their hope of eternal life will always say about their service to God, "This is the only way I can live. I know the Lord forgives me for the sake of his Son. But if I refuse to seek glory and honor and immortality by patiently doing good, I will face God's judgment."

Abraham in the New Testament

Hebrews 11:17-19

The writer to the Hebrews gives us insights into what Abraham was thinking when he raised the knife to sacrifice his son.

> [17] By faith Abraham, when he was tested, offered Isaac. This man, who received the promises, was ready to offer his only son, [18] about whom it was said, "Through Isaac

your offspring will be traced." [19] He reasoned that God also had the ability to raise him from the dead, and in a figurative sense, Abraham did receive him back from the dead.

Isaac was not a son whom God could replace. God had named Isaac as the heir of the promise who would be in the line of the Savior. This verse explains what Abraham was thinking when God told him to sacrifice Isaac. God would not simply replace Isaac with another son. Rather, he would raise Isaac from the dead.

What we learn about Abraham from the New Testament: The writer of Hebrews explains the impossible nature of God's test and how Abraham's faith overcame that impossibility.

The Conversation

These fictional characters reflect on Abraham's test and what they learned from it.

The characters:

Caleb: One of Abraham's servants and a mature believer in the true God.

Chloe: Caleb's wife, also a mature believer in the true God.

Abihu: A man who is somewhat skeptical about Abraham's faith.

Anna: Abihu's wife, who shares Abihu's doubts.

Merit: One of the servants Pharaoh gave to Abraham.

> *Caleb:* But Abihu, didn't you listen to what Abraham just told us in our worship service?

Abihu: Yes, I heard him. But it seems so unfair. Why did God put him through all of that? Abraham has been through so much already. Waiting so long for a son. Then losing Ishmael. And now this. You say it was supposed to be a test?

Anna: Yes. Why did God need to test Abraham? Abraham's been worshipping his God all along. A few slip-ups, maybe. But mostly, Abraham has lived far better than me. Lot is so lucky to have him as his uncle.

Chloe: We're all lucky to have him.

Caleb: Think of everything he's taught us. If it weren't for Abraham, we would all be serving the gods everyone else serves. But now we confess the true God who made heaven and earth.

Abihu: I still ask, "Why did God do this to Abraham?"

Caleb: I'm sure there were times when Abraham thought that, too. The long walk up north. Just him and Isaac, no lamb for a sacrifice. The thoughts he must have had when he looked over at his son!

Chloe: Abihu, that was the test. What would Abraham do if he had to sacrifice the son God had said would inherit the promise of a Savior? The very one! God couldn't just snap his fingers and give him a replacement. With Isaac gone, everything God had told Abraham about Isaac would become a lie. None of it would be true.

Anna: I wouldn't have gone. I would have told God it was impossible. That was immoral. I've heard of some depraved Canaanites sacrificing their children. But Abraham?

CHAPTER 9   Genesis 22

Caleb: Let's think through what Abraham just told us. Abihu, you have to train for battle like the rest of us. Why do we have to wave around such heavy swords? We won't be using them in battle.

Abihu: So we'll become better at using the regular swords.

Caleb: And why does he make us do so many sprints? We won't have to run that far in a real battle, will we?

Abihu: So we'll become faster.

Caleb: Those were tests. Our leader gave us something hard to do so we would become stronger and quicker. And when we've gone through all that work, what does our captain say?

Abihu: He says, Now I know that you are ready. You will do a good job if we are ever attacked.

Caleb: And how does that make you feel?

Abihu: It makes me feel like I've done well. It makes me confident I can face the enemy. And if I pass the final test, maybe I'll get a promotion.

Caleb: Abraham's test was sort of like that. It forced him to rely on God. It made him realize how strong God had made him. And it made him stronger for challenges and temptations to come. God even said that because he obeyed him, he would fulfill his promises to Abraham. So, Abihu, the test was a good thing for Abraham. If it hadn't been impossible, would it have really been a test?

Abihu: I see your point. Maybe that's what God is doing to me sometimes. Sometimes I have to do hard things—nothing like sacrificing my son—but still difficult. Perhaps I should think of them as God's test.

Anna: Maybe I should stop complaining about my problems and ask God to make me stronger. I think I'll pay a little more attention to Abraham when we gather around his altar.

Chloe: His words *will* make you stronger. You can be sure of it. And us too.

Merit: I would like to change the subject a bit. I learned something today that I never realized. Abraham thought that God would raise Isaac from the dead. That was his solution. But God had a different solution. He gave Abraham a ram to sacrifice in Isaac's place.

Caleb: Yes. I wonder if Abraham expected that?.

Merit: Our family in Egypt worships dozens of gods. But I've never heard about one of those gods doing anything like that. They give us good things, or at least their priests say they do. But it's only if we deserve it by giving them something first.

Caleb: Merit, I think Abraham also learned something from this test. Isaac asked his father where the lamb was for the sacrifice. Abraham said that God would provide one. And he did! He provided a ram, which died in Isaac's place.

Merit: A substitute! So that's how Abraham will be a blessing to all nations. The special person to be born from him and Isaac will be *our* substitute.

Chloe: We've all learned from this. We will no longer have to die for our sins.

Caleb: The two lads who went to Mount Moriah came back repeating, "On the Mountain of the Lord it will be provided." I'll have to remember that.

Closing

Micah saw the time when God would fulfill his promise to Abraham. This passage helps us realize that the forgiveness of sins is the heart of God's promise.

Micah 7:16-20
> Who is a God like you, who forgives guilt,
>> and who passes over the rebellion of the survivors
>> from his inheritance?
>
> He does not hold onto his anger forever.
> He delights in showing mercy.
> He will have compassion on us again.
> He will overcome our guilty deeds.
> You will throw all their sins into the depths of the sea.
> You will give truth to Jacob and mercy to Abraham,
>> as you swore to our fathers from days of old.

Chapter 10
Genesis 23; 24; 25:1-8

Abraham Prepares for Sarah's Future—Chapter 23
Abraham Prepares for Isaac's Future—Chapter 24
Abraham Prepares for His Own Future—25:1-8

Prayer: Dear heavenly Father, you have given me many blessings. However, I understand that this world will someday be destroyed. Abraham lived as a stranger in this world, confident that he had a permanent home awaiting him. Help me follow Abraham's example and live with a view to the permanent home I have waiting for me with you. Amen.

Keyword: "Mercy" [32]

Mercy is a good keyword for this final chapter. Mercy refers to God's unwavering, unstoppable, inexhaustible love, which he will never stop showing to those who believe his *covenant* promise of a Savior. In mercy, God is *faithful* to us. In mercy, God reveals his saving *glory* to us. In mercy, God does *what is right* to fulfill his covenant promise. In mercy, God is *just*, forgiving our sins and defending us against our accusers.

When Abraham sent his servant to find a wife for Isaac, the servant prayed for God's blessing. In that prayer, he reminded God of how he had been merciful to Abraham his whole

---

[32] The Hebrew word חֶסֶד is =pronounced KHE-sed." The "e" is short in both syllables. This word is often translated "love."

life.[33] He said, "O LORD, the God of my master Abraham, please give me success this day, and show *kindness* [mercy] to my master Abraham" (Genesis 24:12)

When the servant found Rebekah, Isaac's future wife, he praised God for having given him success: He said, "Blessed be the LORD, the God of my master Abraham, who has not forsaken his *mercy* and faithfulness toward my master. Indeed, the LORD has guided me to the house of my master's relatives" (Genesis 24:27).

When the servant thanked God for *not forsaking* his mercy to Abraham, he was clearly confessing that God had shown mercy to Abraham throughout his life.

In this chapter, we will see that the Lord did not stop showing mercy to Abraham as he grew older.

The Life of Abraham

Abraham Prepares for Sarah's Future—Genesis 23

Abraham prepared for the future. He was not preparing for his own security and ease of life. Instead, he wanted to live with God's promises in mind.

The last time we saw Abraham, he was living in the south of Canaan in Beersheba. In this chapter, we meet Abraham back in Hebron, more to the north. There Sarah died at the age of 127.

---

[33] In these two verses, the EHV translates the word in two ways, "kindness" and "mercy." The word appears another time in the account of Lot. When the Lord, using two angels, was forcing Lot to leave Sodom before it was destroyed, Lot expressed his thanks to the Lord like this: "See now, your servant has found favor in your sight, and you have shown me great *mercy* by saving my life" (Genesis 19:18,19).

CHAPTER 10 Genesis 23, 24, 25 1-8

Abraham had a choice about where to bury Sarah. Perhaps he should bury her in Haran, where the rest of his relatives lived. Returning to Haran, however, would have meant returning to the past. Abraham's future and the future of his descendants lay in Canaan. That is where Sarah should be buried. That's also where he himself would be buried. And that is where others in the line of the Savior would also be buried.[34]

He approached the owners of the land around him, who were Hittites, and asked for a place where he could bury Sarah. The people of the land gave him permission to bury his dead in their territory, and they told him to choose one of their own tombs as a burial place. Abraham said, No. He didn't want to share a piece of property. He wanted to own it outright. He wanted to use the burial place as he chose, without any arguments from the owner.

Abraham was interested in a particular cave, called the Cave of Machpelah, lying in a field owned by a man named Ephron. Like all the Hittites of that area, Ephron considered Abraham to be "a prince of God among us" (Genesis 23:6), so he offered to give Abraham the field for nothing. Again, Abraham said, No. He wanted there to be no question about who owned the property. He wanted to pay full price, and Ephron sold it to him for 400 shekels of silver. A formal transaction took place:

> So the field of Ephron, which was in Machpelah, near Mamre—the field, the cave that was in it, and all the trees that were within the boundaries of the field were deeded to Abraham as his property. This was done in

---

[34] Jacob, Abraham's grandson, would be buried there. So would Abraham's son Isaac and his wife Rebekah, Jacob's wife Leah, and Abraham himself (Genesis 49:29-32).

195

the presence of all the Hittites, who were assembled at the gate of the city. (Genesis 23:17-18)

Abraham then buried Sarah in that cave. Her physical remains would stay in the land that God promised her descendants, even as her spirit was in the land God promises to all who persevere in the faith.

Abraham Prepares for Isaac's Future—Chapter 24

When Abraham looked into the future, he knew his son Isaac would have a child who would be the son of the promise. Abraham set about getting a God-fearing wife for Isaac.

Abraham turned his eyes toward Haran, where his family had stopped after they left Ur of the Chaldees. The family was still there. And unlike the idol-worshipping people of Canaan, Abraham's family knew the true God.

So Abraham sent a servant to Haran to find a wife for Isaac. He had the servant swear an oath to find Isaac a wife from there. There were two conditions. First, if the woman he found did not want to leave her family, the servant must not take Isaac back to Haran to live. And if he could not find a wife for Isaac in Haran, or if the woman would not accompany him to Canaan, he would be released from his oath.

The rest of this account belongs to the life of Isaac, so we won't treat it here. The account is a beautiful example of trust in God and willingness to follow where he leads. The servant was successful. He found Rebekah, brought her to Isaac, and Isaac "loved her" (Genesis 24:67).

CHAPTER 10　Genesis 23, 24, 25 1-8

Abraham Prepares for His Own Future—25:1-8

God blessed the last years of Abraham's life by giving him additional wives and giving him the power to have children. Isaac remained the son of the promise, and Abraham did not want that to be contested by his other sons. They, too, would father large nations. So he gave them gifts and sent them away from Canaan proper and into lands to the east.

Abraham died at 175. Isaac and Ishmael buried him in the Cave of Machpelah, which Abraham had bought from Ephron the Hittite.

Abraham in the New Testament

The New Testament picks up the life of Abraham at this point and tells us where he is spending eternity.

Mark 12:26,27

> [26] But about the dead—that they are raised—have you not read in the book of Moses, in the passage about the burning bush, how God told him, 'I am the God of Abraham, the God of Isaac, and the God of Jacob'? [27] He is not the God of the dead, but of the living.

Matthew 8:11

> [11] I tell you that many will come from the east and the west and will recline at the table with Abraham, Isaac, and Jacob in the kingdom of heaven.

Abraham is not dead. He has risen from death and now lives with God.

Luke 16:23

> ²³ In hell, where he was in torment, [the rich man] lifted up his eyes and saw Abraham far away and Lazarus at his side.

In the story of the rich man and poor Lazarus, the rich man saw Lazarus in Heaven, sitting at Abraham's side.

Hebrews 11:8-10; 13-15

> ⁸ By faith Abraham obeyed when he was called to go to a place that he was going to receive as an inheritance, and he left without knowing where he was going. ⁹ By faith he lived as a stranger in the Promised Land, as if it did not belong to him, dwelling in tents along with Isaac and Jacob, who were heirs with him of the same promise. ¹⁰ For he was looking forward to the city that has foundations, whose architect and builder is God.
>
> ¹³ One by one, all of these died in faith, without having received the things that were promised, but they saw and welcomed them from a distance. They confessed that they were strangers and pilgrims on the earth. ¹⁴ Indeed, people who say things like that make it clear that they are looking for a land of their own. ¹⁵ And if they were remembering the land they had come from, they would have had an opportunity to return. ¹⁶ Instead, they were longing for a better land—a heavenly one. For that reason, God is not ashamed to be called their God, because he prepared a city for them.

God called Abraham to leave Haran. Abraham obeyed and went, even though he didn't know where God was taking him. When he entered Canaan, God told Abraham that this was the land he would give to his descendants. With that promise, Abraham had no desire to return to Haran.

Moreover, he was content to live in Canaan like a temporary visitor. He was willing to live in tents because he knew he had a permanent home waiting for him in Heaven.

This pictures what God has called all his followers to be. God has called us out of this world. Our residency here is temporary. Even though our homes do not match the grandeur of the houses owned by the citizens of the world, we are content with whatever God gives us. We have no desire to go back and live in the world. We are looking forward to the most wonderful home imaginable—a permanent home in Heaven designed and built by God himself.

Sometimes we comment on the lack of details Abraham and the other Old Testament believers had about the coming Savior. But that didn't make their faith less specific and less sure. We might compare this to our hope of Heaven. We don't know much about our eternal home. And we find ourselves unable to answer questions about what it will be like there. But that doesn't make our faith in Heaven vague and uncertain. We know that Heaven awaits us with the same degree of certainty that Abraham had when he looked forward to the birth of the promised Savior.

What we learn about Abraham from the New Testament:
We learn that Abraham obeyed God and left Haran, even though he did not know where he was going. On earth, he was content to live in tents because he knew his home in Heaven would be a permanent home. Like all the Old Testament believers, he had no desire to return to the worldly way of life out of which he had been called. And now he is in the permanent home he had been waiting for.

The Conversation

The characters are fictional, as is the conversation. But it speaks about real happenings in Abraham's life.

The Characters:

Caleb: One of Abraham's servants and a mature believer in the true God.

Chloe: Caleb's wife, also a mature believer in the true God.

Merit: One of the servants Pharaoh gave to Abraham.

> *Caleb*: Here we are, a little group, living like strangers in a land that doesn't belong to us, trying to hold on to our faith in the true God when everyone else is worshipping idols. It seems we are just holding on. But look at what the Lord has accomplished here through Abraham.
>
> *Chloe*: As soon as we got here, Abraham began to build altars and worship God. And he didn't hide them away in a big tent. Even if we had a big tent, it wouldn't hold all of us. There we were, out in the open. Once in a while, I saw some curious Canaanites, wondering what we were doing.
>
> *Merit*: Abraham wasn't perfect. He was scared of the people in Egypt—and there are a few people around there that I'm scared of too. But look what happened. God used Abraham's weakness to bring some Egyptians to faith. My family and I are good examples. It was hard to leave Egypt, but it was a blessing to become part of Abraham's household. We came to know the true God. And there must be many more like us. I don't know

about Pharaoh, but I can imagine that there are others in Pharaoh's household whom God brought to faith.

Caleb: And think of all the people around Hebron whom Abraham influenced. He had some good friends, Mamre, Aner, and Eschol. What interesting conversations he must have had with them. And think about their soldiers. They witnessed Abraham's trust in God and his bravery in the battle with the four kings.

Chloe: And think of the people with him when he returned from the battle and met Melchizedek. They must have been surprised when he blessed Abraham and Abraham gave him a tithe. They were hearing things they had never heard before.

Caleb: And when Abraham gave all the plunder back to the people of Sodom, what must they have thought? I wasn't too happy with that. But Abraham explained what he was doing, and he showed us how important God's promises were to him.

Merit: I keep thinking about the people of Sodom whom Abraham rescued. They all saw Abraham's power. They must have asked Lot about what made him so brave. They had so many opportunities to learn about the true God. God gave them every chance to turn from their wicked ways. But they ignored it all. And how much they suffered.

Chloe: Think about what just happened. The people of Hebron had a chance to work with Abraham when he was looking for a place to bury Sarah. If I wanted to give someone a piece of land but he insisted on paying for it, I would surely wonder why.

Merit: And I think of what happened in Gerar in the Philistine territory. It was no different from Egypt. Abraham lied about Sarah to Abimelek. And he suffered as a result. But through it all, people were blessed. Abimelek learned that Abraham was a prophet and could pray for him. What else must he and Phicol have learned from this man?!

Caleb: And there were likely many others who came to know the Lord and his promise of a Savior—people we don't even know about. As Eliezer often reminds us—that day when God told Abraham that his descendants would be like the stars in the sky, Abraham believed God's promise and it was credited to him as righteousness. Again, the substitute God will provide for us comes to mind. Like Abraham, we are righteous in God's eyes through faith him.

Chloe: We are strangers in this land, but we are not hidden from the owners of the land among whom we live.

Caleb: Someday, Abraham will own this land. But in the meantime, in how many ways will its present owners be blessed by us strangers? I'll remember Abraham for that, too.

Closing

As you read this response, focus on God's righteousness. God will destroy the world, but in righteousness he will bring his people into the new Promised Land.

Isaiah 51:1,2,5,6

    Listen to me, you people who pursue righteousness,

you people who seek the Lord!
Look confidently to the rock from which you were
> hewn
>> and to the quarry from which you were cut.
Look confidently to Abraham your father,
> and to Sarah, who gave birth to you.
Yes, when I called him, Abraham was only one person,
> but I blessed him and multiplied him. . . .
My righteousness is near.
My salvation goes forth,
> and my arms will bring justice to the peoples.
The seacoasts will wait for me.
They will have confidence in my arm.
Lift up your eyes to the heavens.
Look closely at the earth beneath,
> because the heavens will vanish like smoke,
> and the earth will wear out like a garment,
> and its inhabitants will die like gnats.
But my salvation will remain forever,
> and my righteousness will never be abolished.

Summary

"The Conversation"

The important episodes in Abraham's life are the ones Moses chose to include in Genesis. But the conversations brought up issues likely discussed by the people in Abraham's camp.

- Abraham's occasional doubt and his lies about Sarah definitely had an impact on some of the servants. No doubt, they had to deal with those sins just as we today deal with the sins of others.
- The believers among them must have realized how privileged they were to be Abraham's servants and how much they learned from his words and examples.
- The details God gave Abraham about the future of his descendants were likely on the minds of Abraham's descendants, especially during the years when Jacob and his family lived in Egypt.
- The believers in Abraham's camp were not to be like the people in Canaan. But they likely interacted with them and may have led some to know the true God.
- Abraham was a visitor in the land of Canaan. But occasionally he was a very active part of the community. The servants might have discussed that fact

and the influence that Abraham had on the people around them.

"The Life of Abraham"

The qualities that please God are all on display in the life of Abraham.

- Jesus' words describe the one characteristic that Abraham's life embodied from beginning to end. Abraham looked forward to the Savior. He knew that the Savior would come from his descendants, and so his faith in God's promise of a son was credited to him as righteousness.
- Jesus described Abraham to the Jewish people: "Your father Abraham rejoiced that he would see my day. He saw it and was glad" (John 8:56). Abraham showed his joy in the coming Savior when he honored Melchizedek, who pictured the Savior.
- When God commanded Abraham to do difficult things, God first gave him promises. Abraham relied on those promises, and they shaped his actions. This is true when he set out for Canaan at God's command, when he was willing to sacrifice his son, Isaac, and when he chose a place to bury Sarah.
- Abraham showed his willingness to obey God by immediately circumcising the males in his household when God commanded him to do so.
- Abraham showed his hatred of idolatry by insisting that his son marry a woman from his family in Haran rather than a woman from the idol-worshipping people living around them in Canaan.
- Abraham's faith led him to be generous. He had no doubt that he would always be blessed, as God had

- promised. He showed his faith in this promise when he let Lot choose the best grazing land.
- Abraham loved the Lord. He openly expressed this love when he built altars and praised God's name. And when he did this, he was also helping others come to know the Lord.
- His love for his fellow believer, Lot, led him to risk his life to save Lot from captivity, and later to pray that God deliver him from Sodom's destruction.
- On two occasions Abraham faltered in his trust. God forgave him and even protected him against the men he had sinned against. He also faltered when he tried to fulfill God's promise by having a child by Sarah's servant, Hagar. Yet God forgave him for that also, and he richly blessed his son by that union.
- Abraham spent his days faithfully caring for his family and household, and quietly fulfilling the vocation to which God had called him. His greatness lay in his humble trust in God, not in the results of his own ambitions.
- Abraham is the father of all who share his faith. As his children, we find in Abraham a model for our faith and life.

"Abraham in the New Testament"

The key to understanding Abraham's life lies in the New Testament. The large number of times Abraham is referred to in the New Testament attests to that.

Jesus and the New Testament writers teach us how Abraham serves as an example of a person who lived in service to God. But what they were most interested in was Abraham's faith. Although Abraham lived in Old Testament times, his faith serves as a model for the faith of New Testament believers. Here is a list of the truths we have gleaned from the New Testament about Abraham's life and faith—truths that still teach us today.

- Abraham is the person from whom God's Old Testament people are descended. (Matthew 1:1,2)
- Jesus was the center of Abraham's life. He looked ahead and rejoiced when he saw the Savior's birth. (John 8:56)
- The promises God made to Abraham were not just for his own descendants. The whole world would be blessed through him. This is the Gospel message we believe, namely, that one of Abraham's descendants was born to save the world from sin. (Acts 3:24-26; Galatians 3:8,9)
- Abraham trusted God and obeyed him. He obediently left Haren when God told him to, and he let God lead him to wherever he wanted. (Hebrews 11:8)
- Abraham showed hospitality to strangers who showed up at his door one day. In this, he also serves as our example. (Hebrews 13:1-3)
- Abraham was content to live in tents as a stranger in Canaan, and he had no desire to return to Haran, even though he might find a more stable and pleasant life there. He considered himself a visitor in the land of Canaan and had a permanent home awaiting him in Heaven. God wants all people to have this attitude toward life in this world. (Hebrews 11:9-16,17)
- Abraham understood that Melchizedek was a special king and priest who prefigured Christ, the

great King and High Priest. Melchizedek blessed Abraham, and Abraham gave Melchizedek a tenth of the plunder from the battle he had just fought. Both these acts showed that Jesus' priesthood was greater than the Old Testament priesthood that came from Abraham. (Hebrews 7:1-11;17)

- Abraham teaches us that we are not saved by keeping the Law, but through faith in the promise. (Galatians 3:6-9; Romans 4:1-4)
- Since Abraham was not righteous because he did God's will, but through faith in God's promise, God's blessing was a matter of grace and was guaranteed to him and to all Abraham's offspring who share his faith. (Romans 4:13-17)
- Abraham believed that God would give life to his and Sarah's dead bodies so they could have a son. In the same way, we believe that God gave life to his dead Son and raised him from the grave after he had won righteousness for all people. (Romans 4:17-25)
- In addition to the gospel promise, God gave Abraham the covenant of circumcision. The sequence of Abraham's life helped the early church sort out the place of circumcision in a Christian's life, if any. Abraham received circumcision long after God gave him promises by grace and declared him righteous through faith. Abraham's example taught the early church that Jews and Gentiles are saved in the same way, namely, through faith in the Gospel. Circumcision was primarily a sign of the righteousness Abraham had by faith. It applied for a time, passed away along with all the Mosaic laws when Jesus

came, and plays no role in a Christian's life. (Romans 4:9-11; Galatians 3:13-18)
- Abraham is the spiritual father of all believers. He is the father of his own physical descendants who share his faith and walk in his footsteps. And he is the father of non-Jews who share his faith and serve God as he did (Romans 2:25-29; Romans 4:11,12,16).
- Neither the law of circumcision nor any of the other laws God gave to his people changed the promise God had originally given to Abraham. (Galatians 3:17,18)
- Abraham served as a pattern of faith and life. Following that pattern makes us children of Abraham (Galatians 3:26-29 and many other passages in the New Testament).
- The promises God gave to Abraham are the fountainhead of the faith of God's Old Testament people. These promises provide direction to our reading of the Old Testament. (Luke 1:41-55; 68-75).
- Abraham knew that when he died, he would go to Heaven and live in a "city that has foundations." We have the same hope awaiting us. (Hebrews 11:9)
- Both Abraham and Sarah lived by faith in God's promises, and through faith they received the ability to have a child, even though such a thing was impossible for them, humanly speaking. (Hebrews 11:11)
- Abraham tried to fulfill God's promise by having a son with Sarah's maid, Hagar. Paul used this account as an example of trying to be saved by human plans and methods instead of by trusting in God's. Salvation by deeds leads to slavery; salvation through

> Christ's righteousness leads to freedom. (Galatians 4:21-31)
- God told Abraham to do an impossible thing, namely, to kill the very person whom God had said would be in the line of the Savior. Abraham trusted that God would find a way out of this impossible situation. God sometimes tells us to do impossible things to test us. By doing this, he gives us a chance to rely on his wisdom and power. (Hebrews 11:17-19)
- Like Abraham, Sarah is an example of someone who had faith in God's promises and whose faith enabled her to have a son well past the normal time for childbearing. (Hebrews 11:11) She also gives us an example of a wife whose obedience to her husband was pleasing to God. (1 Peter 3:6)
- Abraham is still alive and living with God in Heaven. (Mark 12:26,27; Hebrews 11:10-15) We will someday join him there. (Matthew 8:11)

We saw Abraham and Sarah commit sins, and there are lessons we can learn from their weaknesses. Surprisingly, however, the New Testament never mentions those sins or uses them to teach us. It only uses Abraham's and Sarah's faith and their God-pleasing deeds.

Although Abraham lived two thousand years before Christ, he is the father of us all. He teaches us to follow God's direction and shape our lives around his promises. And most importantly, he teaches us everything we need to know about the Gospel message and about salvation through faith in Christ's life and death.

"Keywords"

The account of Abraham is primarily an account about the LORD. It is about his *glory* in promising a Savior and in seeing that promise through to completion (Chapter 1).

This is the meaning of God's *righteousness*. Everything God did was the right thing to do to fulfill his promise (Chapter 2). In the life of Abraham, that word takes on added importance. Melchizedek, the king of righteousness, pictures Jesus, whom God sent to win "the gift of righteousness" for all people (Chapter 3). And just as Abraham believed the Lord's promise and it was credited to him as righteousness, so everyone who believes that Christ acquired the gift of righteousness for them is credited with righteousness through faith alone (Chapter 4). Finally, those who are righteous through faith serve God by living righteous lives (Chapter 9).

Abraham lived under God's *covenants*. For the first ninety-nine years of his life, Abraham lived under God's one-way promise covenant. Shortly before God gave him a son, Abraham was made to live under another covenant, the covenant of circumcision. This was a two-way covenant, which Abraham obeyed as a sign of the righteousness he had by faith. This did not replace God's promise of a Savior, and salvation always came through him (Chapter 5). God's *judgment* is perfect. He punishes those who reject the Savior (Chapter 6) and, for the Savior's sake, he blesses those who believe in him (Chapter 7). God is also *holy*. He is set apart from human idols and does not treat us as our sins deserve (Chapter 8). God is always *merciful* to us for Jesus' sake and directs our lives in his loving kindness (Chapter 10).

Closing

When we study the life of Abraham our minds are always on Jesus—just like Abraham was glad when he looked into the future and saw his coming. His thoughts paralleled those of the psalmist:

Psalm 72:1,2;17-19

> God, give your authority to judge to the King.
> Give your righteousness to the Son of the King.
> He will judge your people with righteousness.
> He will judge your afflicted ones with justice.
>
> May his name endure forever.
> May his name flourish as long as the sun.
> They will be blessed through him.
> All nations will call him blessed.
>
> Blessed be the LORD God, the God of Israel,
> > who alone does marvelous deeds.
> Blessed be his glorious name forever.
> May the whole earth be filled with his glory.

Scripture Index

Genesis
3:15 16
8:1 4
11:32 7
12:1 1
12:1-3 11
12:2-3 105
12:2,3 14, 98
12:3 37, 72
12:6 15
12:7 15
12:7,8; 13:18 44
12:8 16, 19
12:16 40
12:17 30
13:4 44
13:7 39
13:9 38
13:13 39
14:14 14
14:19 58
14:20 58
14:19,20 54
14:22 5
15 77
15:1 66
15:1-6 73
15:2 66
15:4 30, 66, 83
15:5 73, 84
15:6 67, 68, 166, 168
15:8 75
15:14 79
15:15-18 166
15:16 39, 77 112
15:17 77
15:18-21 77
16:2 5
16:3 66
16:16 14
17:5 72
17:9,10 16
17:10 87
17:12 16
17:14 94
17:15,16 31
17:17 93
17:18 31
17:19 31, 93
17:26,27 94
18:13,14 116
18:15 116
18:17-19 121
18:20,21 112
18:24,25 129
19:18,19 194
20:1 32
21:6-7 151
21:10 152
22:2 162
22:7 163
22:8 162
22:11-18 167
22:12 164, 167, 172
22:15-18 164
22:16 166
22:18 166, 186
23:6 195
23:17-18 196
24:1ff 8
24:12 5, 194
24:27 194
24:50,51 5, 10
24:67 196
26:4-5 166
27:46 8
29:1-30 8
31:25ff 11
31:34,35 9
35:2-4 9
49:29-32 195

Exodus
6:2-8 4
6:5 4
34:6,7 5

Numbers
13:17-20 40
13:28-31 15
13:30 41

Deuteronomy
10:16 100
30:6 101

Joshua
2:8-13 172
24:2,3 9
24:12 52
24:14 10

1 Samuel
2:1,2 143

2 Samuel
18:18 53

1 Chronicles
16:8-18 80
16:15-16, 18-22 13
16:18-28 23
16:20-22 151

2 Chronicles
3:1 163
20:7 173

Nehemiah
9:7,8 166

Esther
2:12,13 30

Psalms
33:16-18 53
36:5-12 28
40:9,10 27
48:9-11 127
103:2-6 127
105:37-45 108
110 57, 62, 63
110:4 55
144:1 51

Isaiah
5:16 143
6:3 143
6:7 143
6:8 143
29:18-24 159
29:22-23 11
30:15-18 127
41:8,9 173
41:8-13 138
42:1-4 128
42:6-8 26
51:1,2,5,6 202
55:1-5 144
64:4-9 183
64:6 182

Jeremiah
2:35 113
4:4 101
9:23,24 128
10:23,24 129
33:23-26 124

Ezekiel
7:2-4 113
24:14 113

Daniel
9:4-10 185
10:11-12 185

Micah
7:16-20 191

Matthew
1:1,2 152, 208
3:7-9 101
5:5 71
5:7 89
5:17-20 181
6:12,14,15 181
8:11 197, 211
25:20-21 174
25:21 180
25:31-46 175
25:40 177

Mark
12:26,27 197, 211

Luke
1:41-55; 68-75 210
1:52-55 116
1:68-79 117
3:8 103
13:16 102
16:23 198
17:26-33 135
19:9 102
22:19-20 91

John
7:22 94
8:31-40 102
8:56 67, 206, 208
8:56-58 19
14:21 174
15:10 174

Acts
3:24-26 19, 208
7:2-4 7
15:1 89
15:8-11 96
15:10-11 89

Romans
2:5 114
2:6-11 177
2:13 171, 173
2:25-29 99, 210
3:8 171
3:21 178
4:1-4 209
4:1-5 70
4:1-5; 13-25 70
4:5 71
4:9-11 96, 210

4:11,12,16 99, 210
4:13-17 71, 209
4:17 72
4:17-22 73
4:17-25 209
4:18 73
4:23-25 73
5:16 114
8:11-14 180
9:4,5 97
9:6-9 104

1 Corinthians
5:9-10 135
15:58-58 182

2 Corinthians
5:10 114, 178

Galatians
2:20 181
3:6-9 69, 209
3:8,9 208
3:13-18 97, 210
3:17,18 210
3:19 88
3:26-29 210
4:21-31 153, 211
5:6 177

Colossians
2:17 89

Hebrews
6:13-20 169
6:15 169
6:17 169
6:18 169
6:19 169

7:1-9,17 55
7:1-11;17 209
7:11,17 60
10:24 185
11:4 17
11:5,6 17
11:7 18, 164
11:8 20
11:8-10; 13-15 198
11:9 210
11:9,10,13-16 43
11:9-16,17 208
11:10 136
11:10-15 211
11:11 156, 210, 211
11:17-19 186, 211
12:18-21 92
12:22-24 92
13:1-3 116

James
2:14 170
2:14-17 170
2:18-20 170
2:20-24 169
2:21-24 172
2:25,26 172
2:26 172

1 Peter
3:6 102, 211

2 Peter
2:6-9 133
2:7-9 38

References to Abraham in the New Testament

Matthew 1:1-17
Matthew 3:7-9
Matthew 8:11
Mark 12:26,27
Luke 1:52-55
Luke 1:68-75
Luke 3:8
Luke 13:16
Luke 16:23
Luke 17:26-33
Luke 19:9
John 7:22
John 8:31-40
John 8:51-58
Acts 3:24-26
Acts 7:2-4
Acts 13:26
Romans 4:1-25
Romans 9:6-9
Galatians 3:6-9
Galatians 3:13-18
Galatians 3:26-29
Galatians 4:21-31
Hebrews 6:11–7:9;
Hebrews 7:17
Hebrews 11:8-19
Hebrews 13:1-3
James 2:18-26
1 Peter 3:6
2 Peter 2:6-9

www.ingramcontent.com/pod-product-compliance
Lightning Source LLC
Chambersburg PA
CBHW060130190426
43200CB00039B/2656